Why Church Buildings Matter

The Story of Your Space

Tim Cool

Published by Rainer Publishing
www.rainerpublishing.com

ISBN 978-0615951812

Printed in the United States of America

Contents

Chapter 1

The Church Building as Story

Life is best understood through a story – God's story. It is a story that transcends and explains our experiences, our questions, our deepest yearnings, our greatest hurts. It is about God the person. His passion. His hopes. His heart. It is a story that includes a cherished beloved, a seductive villain, a hero's journey, and a broken heart. It begins with "Once upon a time" and ends with "happily ever after." It is a story within which our own can be told.
- Kurt Bruner, *The Divine Drama*

Over the past several years we have become acutely aware of the essence of "story." We hear this term used in the church world and in business settings. It has been used to prompt people to open up about their lives and life experiences...to tell their story. On a corporate level it is the interwoven thread used to identify the mission, vision, direction, and passion of organizations. The reality is, we all have a story. Some of these stories are sensational while others may seem mundane or routine. Others grip our emotions and pull on our heartstrings while transforming us into the story.

What has struck me lately is that everyone has a story to tell and that people are reading—taking in—those stories even when we are not aware. We do not have to write a screenplay or book to tell our story. When we walk into a room full of people, you will start to read certain aspects of people's stories, and they will start to read yours as well. They might not see the entire story, but they will see some pretty obvious chapters in that story. The way you enter the room will tell the chapter of your story related to your self-confidence or possibly your physical attributes or limitations. The way you shake the hands of the other guests will convey yet another part of the story, as will the clothes you are wearing...and you may not have even said a word. In addition, the room itself tells a story (more on that later).

The concept of storytelling has become an "ah ha" moment for me. I have learned that some of the most interesting, complex, intuitive, and compelling parts of my story are those observed and not heard. If I have to verbally communicate that a component of my story is generosity and kindness, then it is very likely that thoseattributes are not really part of my non-fiction story, but rather a fictional (fairy tale) trait that I want people to believe about me. Life stories are generally seen and felt long before they are verbally communicated. In fact, I believe that some parts of our story, those with the most intrinsic value, are never spoken. We did not need to hear Mother Theresa tell us she loved orphans. Michael Jordan doesn't need to give a speech on why he's one of the most captivating athletes to play the game. We do not need to have a mother, rocking her baby, to tell us that she loves that gift from God. No, we can see it. We can feel it. There is something that communicates the story to us just by looking at the person or the situation.

At a recent conference in Seattle, Andy Stanley took what we call "story" and added a brand new twist to it. He calls it the "setting", which refers to the physical environment—the landscape and the building. People intuitively feel their setting and make judgments about it, even subconsciously. This setting reiterates the fact that design matters... the little details matter... the cleanliness of the facility matters... organization matters... safety matters... decor and colors matter... presentation matters... content matters. And why? Because people matter and these things are important to people.

Andy went on to say:

> The church is a bunch of environments. Staff and volunteers are from various church backgrounds. Every person that shows up to do ministry has a picture in their head of what a win should be. The problem is that if everyone doesn't have the same "win" in mind it creates problems. You need to develop 3-5 win definitions of your own. North Point is unapologetically attractional. If Andy could heal people at will like Jesus did, he would. He cannot. Instead he can do great children's ministry and have a great band. Highlight the word "crowd" in the book of Mark. Everywhere Jesus went he was surrounded by people who couldn't get enough of him. Jesus was attractional.

I believe he's right. Church facilities and all of the things associated with "story" and "setting" will not save a person from a life of sin and frustration. But the lack of attention to these things can indeed be the road block to reaching those people that need to hear the gospel message the most. Don't minimize their impact. That would be a huge mistake.

"Story" is all around us, in virtually every aspect of our daily experiences, which means that our church and ministry facilities also tell a story. Here are a few important questions to ask about your church facilities:

What story are your facilities/campus telling?

Are we intentional about the telling our story through our facilities?

Is the story congruent with who we are, who we think we are, what we believe and value, and who we want to reach for Christ?

In the following chapters of this book, we will explore each of these areas in more detail. I believe as we become more acutely aware of the impact of our ministries' unique stories, and how it impacts our guest and the people God has called us to reach in our community, the greater the impact we will have on fulfilling our calling.

Chapter 2

The Power of Story and Place

Storytelling is likely the oldest art form, and may still be the most powerful one. Story is how—long ago—we learned to take the confusing realities and concepts of many things that happen and try to make sense of them. A story is a fundamental way that humans organize and store information.

When a story takes shape, we've taken that string of events and invested it with meaning. What was important enough to shape into a story and to tell others about it? When something had meaning. We desire meaning, and will likely try to create it whenever and wherever we can. The human connection is based in story. And story creates and leads culture.

According to Ursula K. Le Guin, writing in *The Language of the Night*, "The story—from *Rumpelstiltskin* to *War and Peace*—is one of the basic tools invented by the mind of man, for the purpose of gaining understanding."

Mark Twain agreed. His first rule of writing was "that a tale shall accomplish something and arrive somewhere."

A story *must* go somewhere. It follows, with purpose, one or more characters through a series of events. By the end, it arrives at a target destination, reaching its target audience, fulfilling its reason for having been told.

The theology of story is fascinating to me. Story has been called "the way we explain the world to ourselves" and "the way we explain ourselves to ourselves." Story has been also referred to as a "waking dream" in which we reframe our lives in symbol and metaphor to find meaning.

To make it understandable, we can define story simply as a narrative or a visual sequence of events. Something happens, and that leads to something else, and that leads to something else.

Storytelling is the mindful sharing of experience and imagination in an understandable form.

Let's break that down.

"Mindful sharing" means intentionally telling a story with a purpose in mind.

"Experience and imagination" are placeholders for the emotional timbre of the story that resonates with the audience.

"Understandable form" means using a familiar story structural format for the series of events. What will the reader or observer be able to relate to and understand?

There are lots of kinds of stories and different ways of communicating them. It's necessary, because if everybody liked the same thing then we would be robots, living a non-creative life, in a boring state of Generica (more on that topic later). God is creative. If we take the time to just sit in a park for any length of time, we can see how creative he is. Observe the flowers, shape of trees, topography of the land, sounds, smells, cool breezes, shade, sun, and insects. When was the last time you went to a zoo? Talk about creativity! When you see the flat-billed platypus, hippo, toucan, blue dragon sea slug, Gunnison grouse, peacock worm, star-nosed mole, and of course, the sucker-footed bat. God did not create the earth and all of its creatures to be the same. He did not intent their dwelling places to be the same either.

When we think in terms of story, we must also think in terms of place. Place and story go hand-in-hand and are interwoven into every aspect of our lives. You can't have story that is not cast in a place. Place does not always have to be a physical place. It can be a virtual place as well as a built environment. Another place is obviously the natural place, God's pallet with which he has provided the most incredible backdrop for storytelling.

The natural place is intrinsic to those wonders of the physical world that thrill and awe us by simply existing. It's the stuff of *National Geographic* specials that create delight through their natural grandeur. Our primary memories of these places will always be the magic of the natural wonders themselves. A subtle balancing and blending act is the key to creating consistent place by showing off the main attraction at its best. I was recently in Colorado Springs and was able to take some alone time to breathe in God's incredible creation. I love the mountains and feel an incredible closeness to God when I am in their midst. Talk about natural place at its best.

My favorite mountain verse is Psalm 121:1 (NLT) – "I look up to the mountains—does my help come from there?" The mountains are the backdrops of God's splendor. In today's culture, the natural place can and should also be an aspect of our built environments. Nature should be considered as facilities are planned, sighted on property and built. Why not use all of the colors, materials, textures and mediums available on the pallet God has blessed us with when we create facilities and tell stories? It's important to know just what tools and resources we have, so that you can put them to work properly. Hammers and screwdrivers are both tools, but they have very different uses.

Built place, similar to natural place should evoke an emotional response as part of our storytelling. Let me re-phrase that: Built place *will* evoke an emotional response. But what type of response? While few manmade places are world icons, even the most mundane can also inspire awe and stir our thoughts and emotions. There are hotels and grocery stores and retailers and automobile dealerships and hospitals and dental offices that stand above others and sparkle. Yes, even churches. People should feel attended to and comfortable in our constructed place.

The third kind of place is that of the virtual place. It demonstrates that place is not always a physical location. Successful organizations must have a presence, a story, and a sense of experience in their virtual world as well as the physical world. The look and feel of our online presence—our digital front porch—must reflect the look, feel, and ambiance of our brick and mortar place. Distinctive and eye-catching design is only the beginning of creating a virtual place; you must also build trust and create a unique experience. From the first click, guests should be drawn in (sucked in), made curious, and delighted by the virtual place you have created.

Caution: Your virtual place cannot represent something totally incongruent to your built place. If it does your guests may feel like they fell for a bait-and-switch tactic. Almost immediately, you can erode trust.

The concepts of story and place are not new concepts, but they seem to be more common vernacular with churches dedicated to reaching their communities and being intentional about communicating their unique stories. It is critical to examine the implication, strategies and contextualization of place and story, and how they can be more than just a ploy or tactic, but rather a critical component to your churches DNA and culture.

We cannot neglect the power of story and how our church facilities communicate a story. As we progress through these chapters, we will address several questions. How does church space support the story? How does the church space prime the heart, minds and emotions of your guests? How does your facility suck people into the story of the church?

Chapter 3

Your Church Facility Should Suck

I realize the play on words is a bit edgy. I want to get your attention. Your church facilities should get the attention of others. In fact, they should suck people in, not repel them away.

Have you ever driven by a park, mall, restaurant or other building that caught your attention and sparked your interest to the point that you just had to pull in and check it out? Maybe it was the design of the building. Maybe it was the look and feel of the campus/grounds. Maybe it was the crowds of people in the parking lots or mingling throughout the campus or possibly it was some other attribute that was so compelling that just sucked you in. There was this innate and unspoken draw that was irresistible. You may have fought the suction the first or second time you passed by, but eventually the gravitational pull and indescribable suction pulled you in like being sucked in by a massive vacuum.

I know I have.

The design of a facility and campus are far more critical in telling your story than most people realize. Road appeal matters. Aesthetics matter. I am not saying that your facility needs to be opulent or look like Westminster Abbey, but it is going to make a statement and tell a story to those in your community. It can also be the catalyst to suck people in or repel them.

I recently attended a national conference aimed at church planters and loved being with thousands of church planters and leaders with a passion to expand the reach of the gospel. But let me give you a common mistake I see many church planters and new churches make far too often.

Church planters will do their due diligence and locate their church in an area of the community that fits their target market. They understand the community and the people they plan to reach. Momentum builds… which leads to growth… which leads to crowded conditions in their rented facility… which leads to buying land… followed by the planning and building of a facility. As with most new churches, money is tight and yet space is needed for ministry. So they find themselves in the conundrum of space vs. dollars. They have bought land in an area of half million-dollar homes right in the heart of their target. But because of their need for cheap space, they throw up an austere structure, most likely a plain-looking metal building. They cut corners on the street scape, landscaping, and entrance signage. Or worse, they put something incongruent with who they are and the community they are trying to reach.

What story have they just told their community? Will people who spent $500,000 plus on their house, that are not yet believers, want to come to the little metal building around the corner? Maybe, but to a passer-by, what are you communicating with your building and campus? Is it appealing? Does it draw (suck) them in? Does it spark a positive emotional reaction? Does it say "Come check us out" without posting a billboard or sign? Does the community see you as an asset or a detriment?

Now, I totally understand the need to have space to fulfill the vision, mission, and ministry of the church. I get the reality that there is a limited budget. These issues are real. What I am suggesting, however, is that we be intentional with our campus and facility design. And intentional does not necessarily mean more expensive. But it does take effort, planning, vision, and vigilance.

We will keep unpacking these factors in the next few chapters. But in the meantime, drive around your community with a set of fresh-eyes. Notice the way some of the facilities and campuses (not necessarily churches) look and see what kind of story they communicate to you. When we are aware that design matters, we start to see things that will cause us to pause and either be sucked in, or merely drive by.

In a recent article by Sam Rainer in *Church Executive* magazine, he lists 10 unexpected trends to surface in 2020. I was particularly taken by this one trend relating to church facilities. This is what Sam said:

> The church is not a building, but a building is where the church meets. And buildings are the most expensive part of discipleship. In North America people go to buildings to do things — they go to the game in an arena, to the doctor at her office, to school in the classroom, and to the movie at the theater. Part of our culture is the expectation that things happen in buildings. This cultural expectation is true of the church — people go to church to be discipled.

Not all churches have buildings, nor am I advocating that they should. But church facilities are one of the most expensive and most critical tools church leaders use in shepherding God's people. In short, buildings are important pieces in God's mission of building his kingdom. Many building and design firms are becoming more intentional about creating space with the purpose of making disciples. In the next ten years, this focus will continue to grow. And churches will begin to view their buildings as part of their discipleship process.

Let those words sink in. Is your local ministry effectively using your facilities as discipleship tools? If so, then you've correctly grasped the primary purpose of a church facility. If not, then what is your primary expectation of your church facility? Is discipleship not your focus or are the spaces not adequate to facilitate spiritual growth? Let's move forward and see.

Chapter 4

Theology, Pragmatism, and Story

We shape our buildings; thereafter they shape us.
- Winston Churchill

Church Facilities and Theology.

The building of monumental cathedrals in the middle ages was a reflection of faith and the channel for much of the creative energy of medieval European society. The dominant feeling was one of great enthusiasm, ambition, and a desire to excel in this quest to construct magnificent buildings reflecting God's glory. Cathedrals were designed to be houses of God, to inspire faith, and to reach to heaven. In a time where the church was the central point of life for both rich and poor, it was natural for the greatest efforts to be made in designing and building the cathedrals. Plus there was the inevitable competitive nature of humans, with each city hoping to have a better cathedral than the others (some things never change).

In addition, many people of the day were unable to read, so the designers and constructors introduced ornamentation and stained glass. In an illiterate world, the use of this art was not just decorative, but it allowed congregants to take in biblical stories visually, as well as the images of the saints to serve as examples. The designer's job in building these edifices was to figure out how to represent best the theology of the church.

This practice of using churches and other houses of worship as theological statements continued for centuries. In the 18th century, the incorporation of steeples became very popular with many church designers. For some it was to express a reaching to the heavens as a form of praise and drawing peoples' eye to God.

So is the church building to make a theological statement? Did the builders of cathedrals get it right or wrong? And why is pragmatism so popular today?

Church Facilities and Pragmatism.

If you have ever studied philosophy, then you are sure to recognize the name William James. James is considered by many to be the most insightful and stimulating of American philosophers. He invented the philosophy of pragmatism. As a professor of psychology and philosophy at Harvard University, he became the most famous living American psychologist and later the most famous living American philosopher of his time (the late 1800's).

So what is a pragmatist and pragmatism? Here are a few definitions:

1. Character or conduct that emphasizes practicality.
2. Action or policy dictated by consideration of the immediate practical consequences rather than by theory or dogma.
3. The doctrine that the contact of concept consists only in it practical application.

In short, it focuses on what works. If something is beneficial and helps accomplish a goal, then it must be true. Something should satisfactorily work in order to be true.

Many church designers and leaders have adopted this approach to their ministry facilities. If we have four walls, a roof, and we can get "x" number of people in the space, then it must be good. If it functionally meets our goals and objectives, then it must be true.

In another article by Sam Rainer, he states:

> James' pragmatism has helped change this [of theology of facilities] philosophy. Most modern church buildings are not theological statements. No longer is the starting point theology, but rather how—pragmatically—people   will experience worship. Function is elevated over theology.

I believe that this is particularly evident when we look at the utilitarian multi-purpose metal building, gymnatorium, cafatorium facilities of the 1980s and 1990s. To me, that is the pendulum swinging too far to the opposite end of the spectrum than that of facilities to depict theology. Facilities should work (pragmatically). But facilities should also say something about God (theologically). Story becomes the connection between church buildings that function well and church buildings that say something about God.

Story - The Best of Both Words.

Is it too far-fetched to think that we can have a facility that functions pragmatically, yet also communicates a story? If the culture of your church, the culture of your congregational makeup, and your target market would be "sucked in" by stained glass that tells stories then by all means, do that. If your DNA and uniqueness is expressed by a different physical manifestation, then do that. There is also no reason that a facility whose physical attributes tell a story cannot also be extremely pragmatic in its function, flow, circulation, and seating arrangement. The key is intentionality, and that intentionality does not have to cost more. The challenge for most pragmatists is that they are just looking for function and are not as likely to take the time to drill down on the vision, mission, values, culture, and story in order to appropriately convey a statement about God in the church building. They think that cost-effective has to be plain in appearance and lacking creativity. That is sad to me.

So why can't we have our cake and eat it too? Theology, story, and cost-effectiveness can all be goals of a church building.

Chapter 5

The Church of Generica

I travel a lot and I am in many cities across the county. One thing that has really struck me is how similar one city is to the next, especially in the 'burbs. Almost every Outback, Chili's, or Applebee's has the same basic design. I can be taken blindfolded into almost any Home Depot or Lowe's, remove the covering and not know what city I am in. In most cases I can be plunked down in a community with developments that are less than 10 years old and much of the architecture of the shopping centers, the so called "urban" housing, and office buildings look very similar.

A part of me feels comfortable and safe, but a deeper emotion wonders if we have settled for a generic mindset and formations. What happened to unique? What happened to original and innovative? Have we commoditized everything to the point that we press them into existence like we were running a Ford assembly line? Have we accepted that we live in "Generica?" If so, are we also content with worshiping at The Church of Generica?

I recently read a blog with the title "Hurdles to Establish Church Innovation." The author starts the article by asking 2 questions:

1. "Does the established nature of some churches hinder innovation?"
2. "Is an established structure antithetical to quick, nimble changes?"

These may seem obvious, but I think they are far more thought-provoking than they may appear on the surface. The article drills down on what is innovation and "established". According to the author, *innovation* is "the process of successfully establishing something new" while *establish* means "to create firm stability." He goes on to poke a couple holes in both by writing:

"Established churches, in particular, can take comfort in the establishment. Traditions and history can easily become a guise for complacency. Innovation can take a back seat to the entrenched processes that help create the stability."

As I read further in to the article, I believe it is communicating a *both/and* scenario. We need to have innovation in all of our ministries. We need to be exploring new and fresh ways to "be the church" instead of getting comfortable with our holy huddles. It may require serious paradigm shifts, and yes, you may very well lose people because of it. If that happens, and you believe that the innovations you have implemented are going to further the Kingdom and the mission of the church, then wish them well and let them go because they may very well have been the limiting factor to you reaching your God-given vision. When we are rejected, many times it is the Lord protecting us from a potentially bad situation or relationship.

At the same time, church plants and new works cannot stay in a mode of only innovating and primarily focusing on being "cool". At some point you need to establish systems, processes, and core values. There needs to be a sense of stability and permanence.

"Generica" can be just as prevalent in a contemporary setting as a 100 year-old traditional church. When I go to a conference of new or cutting edge churches, it strikes me as odd to see many pastors/leaders with the same hair style, same un-tucked shirts, and pointy shoes. Or I will visit a contemporary church to witness the same haze machines, 3 video screens, drum cage, and mono-sloped roof lines. What we think is cool, relevant, and cutting edge can be just as generic as the coat & tie, white columns, red brick, and steeple. This condition is an equal opportunity malady that can infect any church, any movement or any ministry organization.

In the above article, the author continues with 4 hurdles that may be hindering a church from innovating. They are:

1. *Lack of intentionality* - When resources are plentiful, the temptation is to be less intentional. The practice of spaghetti-against-the-wall-and-see-what-sticks is not true innovation. It's haphazard chaos.

2. *Lack of originality* - Innovation is introducing something new, not introducing something with the façade of newness or a new logo.

3. *The wrong metrics* -What gets measured gets done, and what you measure is typically an indicator of what you value. A mature church will measure different things than a new church. However, an overemphasis on the

metrics sustaining the establishment will inevitably deemphasize innovation and dissuade team members from attempting innovation.

4. *The ease of appeasement* - In an established church some leaders prefer the ease of appeasing members rather than innovating to reach new people. Appeasing existing members is much easier than challenging a church to innovate and reach new people.

Avoid becoming the Church of Generica. Innovate! This applies to how you do church, how you reach the community, and yes, how your facilities are designed.

Chapter 6

Generic Ketchup

David Whitting is the Lead Pastor at Northridge Church in Rochester, NY. I had the privilege to work with David and the team at Northridge during the development of their new worship facility several years ago. Since that time, the Lord has greatly blessed the church and David, and me via their ministry and friendship.

David shared a story that I believe is spot on regarding how our facilities communicate and tell stories to our guests. With his permission, the following is his account of his experience with generic ketchup and how it directly applies to our church facilities. Thanks David.

I went out of town Monday and met a great, old friend for breakfast on Tuesday. He took me to his favorite, local breakfast spot - Pete's Diner. We drove up and it looked like a typical diner (not sure what that means to you, but to me it means old, not particularly "shiny" or clean, a bit run down). But that's ok. I wasn't turned off by the outside or inside look of the place. I've been to enough diners to know that doesn't necessarily reflect on the quality of food. But I did get turned off when I sat down and saw the generic ketchup.

When I see generic ketchup at a restaurant, I image this: *If they are willing to save a penny per customer (two pennies at the most) by using generic ketchup and this is one of the most visible foods, then how are they saving money in the kitchen?*

And all of a sudden, I don't want to eat there anymore.

The worst is a restaurant here in my town that I used to go to for breakfast. Not only was it generic ketchup, but the labels were falling off the plastic, generic ketchup bottle. And you'd open the cap to pour out the ketchup and it was obvious that the dried on ketchup around the cap wasn't just a few hours or even days ago. It might be *months* old. In other words, not only were they using generic ketchup, but also they were *refilling* the generic ketchup bottles. I avoid that local diner whenever possible.

And I don't avoid it because I hate generic ketchup.

I'm not sure I can tell the difference. But it tells me something about the restaurant's priorities. And for the first time, while sitting there with my friend, the application to church hit me.

What messages are we sending to new people when we do things with less than excellence? What are the "generic ketchups" in our building (cheap things that we don't even notice anymore)? What message is being received by new people that we aren't intending to send, but we are clearly sending when we save a few bucks and put "generic ketchup" on the table?

Here are a few more thoughts I have on generic ketchup (while thinking of church applications):

I noticed the regulars never notice generic ketchup. They are used to it. It doesn't bother them, and they don't think it should bother new people either. In fact, the management and owners are focused on pleasing the regulars rather than focusing on making the best impression on first-time customers. By doing so they are all overlooking glaring problems.

No one speaks for the first-time customer (guest). If a regular doesn't like something, they will speak up.

If a new customer to the restaurant doesn't like something, they won't say anything. They simply won't return. This one happens in churches all the time!

There are some things that loyal customers are willing to overlook that a new customer may not be willing to overlook.

Even some positive, good changes will causes regular customers to complain, but the changes were helping new customers. Loyal customers may not like a new menu because they knew where everything was on the old one.

Loyal customers tend to be blind to obvious faults that new people see immediately. That could be a smelly entryway (at our family's favorite diner), ripped cushions in the booths, plates and coffee cups that are so old, they look dirty even though they are perfectly clean.

Old and run down might work well for diners, but I don't think it works well for churches. Diners have a nation-wide reputation for being old, run-down, but great prices and great food. Old, run-down yet effective diners are common. Ugly, smelly yet effective churches are not.

Let me give some applications to church life.

First, excellence matters. We often say that excellence honors God and inspires people. I don't think that means you have to spend a lot of money to be excellent.

It simply means that whatever we do, we need to do it well.

We must look at our church facilities through the eyes of new people. At our church, we know that many who walk in our door for the first time are non-believers, new believers, or immature believers. So the look of our facility matters. If they are turned off while checking us out, let it be by the gospel, not because the facility creeps them out a bit.

We tell our new employees and new interns that they are very valuable to us in their first six months because they will see things that we don't notice anymore. They will ask, "Why do you do that?" And sadly, we never thought about how ineffective that was. We try very hard to see everything through a new person's eyes, but once you are no longer new it is difficult to see it through new eyes.

We need to try to get feedback from new people. They will help us see things we don't notice. We likely won't change some or many of them, but being aware of what is hard to swallow for a visitor is very important. For example, we choose to stand and sing for ten to twenty minutes straight every week. It's not visitor friendly, but for the sake of corporate worship, we do it. We feel the tension between balancing corporate worship for God's glory and worship that is attractive to outsiders. Part of balancing this tension is identifying our generic ketchup.

What generic ketchup do you have in your church facility?

Chapter 7

Parables Are For Outsiders

What is a parable? To most of us who have been raised in the church, we have read, re-read and heard teachings on all of the parables of Jesus. Let's look at how a parable is defined:

1. A saying or story in which something is expressed in terms of something else.
2. A short story in which something is expressed in terms of something else.
3. A statement that conveys meaning indirectly by the use of comparison or analogy.

Now with that as our backdrop, let's look at why Jesus told his disciples he used parables. Take a minute and read a couple translations of Mark 4:10-11:

NLT: Later, when Jesus was alone with the twelve disciples and with the others who were gathered around, they asked him what the parables meant. He replied, "You are permitted to understand the secret of the Kingdom of God.

But I use parables for everything I say to *outsiders*.

MSG: When they were off by themselves, those who were close to him, along with the Twelve, asked about the stories. He told them, "You've been given insight into God's kingdom—you know how it works. But to those who can't see it yet, everything comes in *stories*, creating readiness, nudging them toward receptive insight."

There are 2 words (or concepts) that jump out at me. Do you see them and how they apply to this idea of story?

Parables = Stories. It's obvious, but I want to make sure we do not gloss over the fact that Jesus was the greatest storyteller of all time. He used word pictures and mental images to convey the truths of life, love, evangelism, generosity, salvation, forgiveness, mercy, grace, and virtually all of the spiritual gifts. He used culturally relevant stories to communicate His truths so that the listeners/observers could understand it. In fact, while all of the parables in scripture are relevant today to our lives, many reveal an even deeper meaning when we understand the contextualization Jesus was communicating to the specific audience. It is that little nuance that makes a story and storyteller great. Understand your audience and then communicate your story in such a way that will suck them in and deepen their understanding.

Parables were for outsiders. The story helped engage people who were not as connected. Today, this idea of story helps connect people who did not speak church jargon. I would recommend that the word "outsider" is synonymous with what we would call guests in our church world.

In Christ's day, this person may have been devout Jews or the ultra "religious" or just curious passers-by. In any of these cases, they were not yet devoted followers of Christ in a personal way. They may have been religious or criminal. They may have been circumcised at birth or Gentiles. They may have observed all of the rituals and feasts growing up, or they may have worshiped pagan gods...or no gods. They may have been rich or poor, dark or light skin, young or old, male or female. Regardless, they were outsiders regarding a personal relationship with Jesus.

So, who are the "outsiders" in your community? Do parables (or stories) still apply in our approach to reach those people, especially if words are not spoken? If so, then is it really that much of a stretch to want our facilities, campuses, and commons to communicate with stories?

Chapter 8

Peter Drucker, Church Facilities, and the Future of Present Events

Peter Drucker was a futurist and the guru of all things leadership. He was an amazing leader and author, and if you are too young to remember his works, I would recommend you research his writing.

I recently read a blog by Bob Buford, chairman of the board of Leadership Network and author of several bestselling books. In the blog, he referenced Drucker and made the following statement:

Peter always told me that predictions were perilous and inevitably surprising. I have some drink coasters on my desk quoting Peter that say, "The best way to predict the future is to create it." Peter was usually 20 years or so ahead of events. This is the way he explained it to me, "You look out the window to see what is happening today and build your picture of the future by extending the implications of the present."

Did you catch it: "Build your picture of the future by extending the implications of the present." Chew on that just a minute. I'll wait.

OK. Ready to move on?

This statement sparked some thoughts about how it applies to the concept of story we have been exploring. When I first presented the idea that a church facility should suck, I heard from many church leaders. Some were shocked at my use of the word "suck" and others championed the premise.

I want to make sure that all of my readers clearly understand my perspective. So let me elaborate.

I fully believe that a building will never save a soul; it is only a tool. It is a means to an end. But they can be a distraction to some and hinder them from coming on-site and hearing the gospel. Or maybe they come on campus but the condition, flow, aesthetics, and lack of signage become that distraction and they zone out. Environments matter. Settings matter.

The "sucking" that I referred to earlier is what I call architectural evangelism. I have seen it over and over again and heard numerous stories of how someone in the community was drawn onto a campus and later became a Christ-follower. The initial draw was not a "church" or thought of wanting to become a Christian, but something else was compelling them. And that led to the ultimate life-changing experience.

I believe that we need to see the futurity of our facilities. How will our actions today related to design, flow, street appeal, and signage serve us in the future as a tool? Can we envision the future of our present day decisions, or are we only focused on the here and now? That would be sad to me if it were indeed the case. But for many, that is reality.

If we can see our facilities as one of the seeds we sow—just like our words, or actions, or writings—then it adds a whole new perspective to the value of the church facility. I do not want to come across as one who tries to twist scripture to make my point. I have seen too much of that in my life. However, if we can see our facilities as one more seed, then I believe the following scriptures take on a whole new meaning:

Ecclesiastes 11:6 (NLT) "Plant your seed in the morning and keep busy all afternoon, for you don't know if profit will come from one activity or another—or maybe both."

2 Corinthians 9:6 (ESV) – "The point is this: whoever sows sparingly will also reap sparingly, and whoever sows bountifully will also reap bountifully."

Mark 4:26-26 (NLT) "Jesus also said, 'The Kingdom of God is like a farmer who scatters seed on the ground. Night and day, while he's asleep or awake, the seed sprouts and grows, but he does not understand how it happens. The earth produces the crops on its own. First a leaf blade pushes through, then the heads of wheat are formed, and finally the grain ripens. And as soon as the grain is ready, the farmer comes and harvests it with a sickle, for the harvest time has come.'"

Are you willing to see your facilities as one (not the only one, just one) of the seeds you can plant and see how God will bless it to impact your community? Can we see these tools as a both/and strategy as we consider our community impact and outreach? Are we able to see the future of our facility design, function, and "suction" in the present?

Chapter 9

Well Digging vs. Temple Building

The concept is fairly simple and yet profound. It is based on the John 4 passage about the Samaritan woman at the well. Most of us that have been around church for any length of time know this story. We know that Jesus goes to a well in the middle of the day and meets a women with a sordid past and shares life with her by getting a drink of water, physical water, and then offers and provides living water, a relationship. I have heard dozens of sermon applications about this story and I am sure you have as well. So how does it apply to church facility development? This is where it really gets cool.

The concept is that we need to look for opportunities to develop wells on our campuses and within our communities and not just temples. The well is representative of several attributes that I believe the church, as a whole, has not done a great job in providing to our communities. We have been notorious in building temples -- you know, buildings that are used one or two days a week, places that people in our community believe you have to act, look and smell a certain way to enter. A place with too many "thou shalt not" rules, whether they are real or perceived.

A well on the other hand is a part of the community. It represents a place that is a vital part of that culture. In Jesus' time, people came there seven days a week to get water, but also to see their neighbor, get caught up on what was going on in each other's lives, share concerns, and sometimes just hang. They would do life together. Not just on the weekend but every day.

The well was a common place. It was not a place that the community folk would think of when contemplating a place to "meet God." And yet, that is exactly what happened. This common place become a destination were God met a women in need of a Savior, even though that is not what she was looking for the morning as she heading out to gather water. They shared a conversation. They shared a drink of water. They talked about the past, the present, and what the future could be.

All of this happened in an environment that felt "common" to the woman, just the normal place she went every day. But this was an intentional encounter by Jesus. He knew he was going to have this encounter. He used the common place for the extraordinary. This passage tells us that Jesus "had to go through Samaria."

The fact is, from a physical perspective, there were other routes he could have taken to get to Galilee. But he was intentional about going to Samaria, to have this encounter -- to change a life.

But the story of the well did not end there. Notice what else the passage says, "They came out of the town and made their way toward him." The story continued, and the well was a drawing point for other people to come and hear from Jesus.

The women went and told her neighbors that there was something supernatural happening at the well and that they needed to come check it out. And they did. Do you not get excited to see how one common place experience over a glass of water in a non-temple setting led to life changing experience for not only a woman, but for others in her community?

As you think about your church facilities and campus, think about what wells you are providing your community for these kinds of encounters and then be intentional to open yourself up to meet people and start a conversation that could change the world.

Chapter 10

Delta vs. USAir

I fly a lot.

Living in Charlotte, NC, I flew USAir since Charlotte is their primary hub. Most anywhere I want to go is a direct flight. They have a significant number of flights every day to most of the destinations that I fly to. Most of the Charlotte/Douglas International Airport is designed to cater to them and their clientele.

So, why do I almost exclusively fly Delta Airlines? Why would I subject myself to having to fly through another destination?

Let me share some of the reasons why I fly Delta and then we will look at how this applies to the story our church facilities tell:

1. Approximately 80% of my travel is paid for by the clients I serve as part of reimbursable expenses. In light of that, I am constantly looking for the best value I can for our clients, helping

47

them be good stewards. Seeing I generally have to subject myself to a "two-legger" (meaning a connection flight to get to the destination), the flights are less expensive than the equivalent direct flight with USAir. Seeing that stewardship is important to me, it influences my buying and partnering decisions.

2. With the exception of their small CRJ 100/200 planes, every flight has Wi-Fi. If you know me, you know I love my email and connectivity, so I do not mind sitting on a second flight if I can be productive. Our family recently took a vacation that required a 3+ hour flight each direction. We flew USAir as I had significant miles accumulated, and we used them for the trip. We flew a 767 going and a transatlantic 757 on the return. *Neither* plane had Internet service. Grrr! While I was glad not to be "working," I still wanted Internet access for other things like social media, videos, and cloud accounts. My expectations were grossly unmet, and I was frustrated and very disappointed.

3. For the most part, the Delta fleet is newer and better maintained -- or at least they appear to be for the areas of the planes I see. The flights I

mentioned above on USAir were older planes with older decor. Frayed seat upholstery. Worn our carpet. Old seat controls. Retrofitted video monitors. In-flight entertainment systems that did not work or were not activated. If they are not taking care of the areas where paying customers sit for hours, what else are they not maintaining?

4. Flying can be stressful, especially for the infrequent flyer, like my wife and kids, and the majority of the people on a vacation destination flight. So the attitudes, outgoing personalities, approachability, and over all demeanor of the crew, gate agents, and flight attendants is critical. Again, poor marks for our recent experience, and Lisa and I were sitting in first class on the way home. Still, below average customer service compared to what I expected and what I am accustomed to experiencing. It was clear that the first class flight attendant was not invested in her role on this flight. Personal interactions are a direct reflection on the culture, DNA and attitudes of an organization, and this spoke volumes to me.

I could share more about the airline industry pros and cons, but that is not really my point. The point is that the experiences people have as a guest at your church will impact them and can play a significant role in determining if they return as they find their way on their spiritual journey.

First Impressions are so critical, and they tell a story, whether we intend to or not.

Does your church offer an experience that tells a story and is congruent with your mission, vision, and ministry objectives? If not, you may be missing an incredible opportunity to meet the needs of those in your community.

Chapter 11

Who or What Is Your Competition?

I have to admit that I had never given the concept of competition much thought until Mark Waltz addressed it in his book *First Impression: Creating Wow Experiences in Your Church*.

Mark makes the compelling point that as a rule, churches are not competing with another church in town when it comes to reaching the unreached (although those darn Methodists just built a gym which means our youth are going to start going down there. How dare they!), but rather it is everything else that is competing for their attention.

Your first competitor is their bed. Why in the world would a non-Christ follower what to get out of bed to come to your church? What is the motivation? What is the return on their investment of time and energy? When we talk about competition, we must focus on the people we are trying to reach. These are the unchurched, dechurched, and nonbelievers (not sure I like any of these terms but I need to make a point). So, as an unchurched person, why in heaven's name would I want to get out of bed to attend an event at your church on a Sunday morning? The Holy Spirit draws and regenerates a soul. But why would the Holy Spirit draw someone to *your* church? The snooze button should not be a better option than coming to your church.

The second competitor is all of the other things a person can be doing on a Sunday morning. We live in a time-starved culture where it feels like everyone is vying for our attention and time. So as an unchurched person, if I have other things I like to do on Sunday, why prioritize my schedule to provide a time slot for church?

When I was growing up, Sundays were generally a day to rest and relax, even for those that did not go to church. Families would gather together and do life. It was thought inappropriate for sporting teams and leagues to use Sunday as a practice or game day. Not so today. Sunday is just another Saturday, full of this activity, that game, another practice, and so on. I have even read where some school systems are allowing their teams to use Sunday as a practice day. Now, this is not a conversation on the Sabbath and keeping it holy, but it is a reality in our culture that it is harder and harder to convince a time-starved person—who is not a Christ-follower—to give up these other "critical" activities.

The third competitor is every other consumerist activity they experienced that week. Mark articulates that your competition is the experiences and services that the unreached have experienced this past week. Experiences such as the Barista that knows my name and what I drink each morning. How about the dry cleaner that always gets my shirts just right, on time and without buttons missing? Don't forget the great dinner on Friday night where the waiter gets the order right, without writing anything down, and then on top of that the food was cooked just the way I ordered it. That is a great experience.

Harris Teeter is the upper-end grocery store in the Charlotte region. It has some of the nicest and cleanest stores. Imagine that a mom with her kids ventures to Harris Teeter on a Saturday morning to do their weekly grocery run. If the kids are between the ages of 2 and 5 year old, the likelihood of them needing to use the restroom while on this outing is above average.

So, mom takes her preschooler to the Harris Teeter restroom and is greeted with ceramic tiled floors and walls, pleasant odor, a bright lighting, auto-flush, auto-on fixtures, and the latest hand drying apparatus. The trip is pleasant and the mom feels safe, clean and appreciated by the store as a patron. Then on Sunday, she and her family attend a church their neighbor invited them to attend. Again, the preschooler needs to use the restroom. Will they find the same environment as they did Saturday? Will it be as clean and welcoming? If not, which was the better experience for that mom? Will the less than acceptable experience create a desire to return? I think not.

Here is another aspect of this reality. As regular attenders of our churches, we tend to overlook certain items. We step over the piece of duct tape patching the carpet in the foyer. We don't notice the stained ceiling tiles because they have been that way for so long. We walk right past the weeds growing through the sidewalkand the ponding water in the parking lot. We have become desensitized to these items, but I assure you that your first time guests are not. They will notice these things, and their first impression will be impacted by them.

Whether we like it or not, our first time guests are consumers. Your church service is just another event on their calendar of other consumerist events for that week. It is not about God. It is not about religion. It is about an experience, and your facilities will play a major role in that experience. Note, I did not say that your facility "might" play a role. It will.

Will our facilities detract from our guest's first impression? Take some time to walk around your facility with fresh eyes. Maybe even invite a total stranger to walk it with you. It might be telling.

As we continue to explore this concept of story, take the time to start to think about your current or future facilities and how they can be a tool to introduce people to Christ. Not save them, but lower the drawbridge to the community and welcome them in. There are over 300,000 churches in America, and from my estimates over 95% of them have a facility that they either own or have a long-term lease. It means that as believers, we have close to 300,000 storytelling mediums. Is yours one that can make a difference?

Chapter 12

Backstory

*People get addicted to space unless the space
serves a bigger vision.*
- Will Mancini

I think it would be fair to say that the human connection is based on story, which means that story leads culture. But what is culture? We throw that term around as if everyone has the same definition.

Most anthropologists and behavioral scientists would say culture is the full range of learned human behavior patterns. If we, as the church (local and universal), want to influence culture or say our body of believers has a culture, then I think it is important to understand what we are talking about.

In addition, we need to explore the aspects of storytelling that help us communicate our message. Understanding culture begins with vision clarity. Without clarity, your story is going to be more fairy tale than non-fiction. Once you have been able to define culture in your context along with how it relates to your vision, then you can tell your story in a way people understand. Now let's move to what is often called the backstory.

Back-sto-ry
noun

> *1. A narrative providing a history or background context, especially for a character or situation in a literary work, film, or dramatic series.*

> *2. Similar background information about a real person or thing that promotes fuller understanding of it.*

In virtually every literary work, film, movie, drama, Broadway show, or video game, a backstory is developed before the main story is ever told. It is the foundation of the story. It is the unwritten, unseen, and sometimes unknown reason for the story. It is historical facts that explain why the hero in the story is so shy or bold or rugged.

When considering developing a literary work, backstory is the life of the character that occurred prior to the start of the story. Backstory is the foundation upon which a writer knows his or her character as intimately as you might know your child, lifelong friend, or spouse. Main characters typically have very detailed backstories, while backstories for secondary characters might be more general.

Our experiences to date make us who we are. The people we've known and events we have gone through, good and bad, shape our emotional and intellectual characters. They help to define our abilities, challenges, and especially our choices. Creating a main fictional character that is believable and compelling requires giving that character such a history, a biography that encompasses every major event and influence that has affected the character.

Although backstory can take as much work to build as the story itself, it does not typically appear in the story. Instead we see the effects of backstory by watching the character act and react to events. Developing the backstory to best describe the culture, DNA, vision and mission of your church can be time consuming but is a necessary part telling your story.

There are several concepts that the backstory must address when we consider our unique story:

1. Culture and the church
2. Vision clarity
3. Contextualization
4. Congruency
5. Intentionality

Let's start to unpack each of these concepts in the next chapters.

Chapter 13

Culture and the Church

If a church leader attempts to implement a strategy without first addressing the culture, the strategy is doomed before it even launches.

- Eric Geiger

What is culture? The term was first used to describe the full range of human behavior by the pioneer anthropologist Edward B. Tylor in his book, *Primitive Culture,* published in 1871. Tylor defines culture as "that complex whole which includes knowledge, belief, art, law, morals, custom, and any other capabilities and habits acquired by man [and women] as a member of society."

If Tylor correctly depicts culture, then we must consider the following statements:

1. My country has a culture.
2. The state where I live has its own culture.
3. The city where I live has its own culture.
4. My neighborhood has its own culture.

5. My church and other organizations in my community have their own culture.

Now, there is undoubtedly some overlap between each of these cultures. The culture of my city and state may have certain traits that overlap each other as well as my local community and neighborhood. Yet there are going to be nuances that make them uniquely different.

Culture is how people in a community live. It includes their ideas, language, religion, and history. It includes the clothes people wear and what they learn in school. Every community in the world has a culture. Children learn about culture from their families, and when they get older, they pass on this culture to the next generation.

All cultures are alike in some ways because all people have the same basic needs. All people communicate. How they communicate depends on their culture. People in different cultures use different languages. All people need shelter. The kind of shelter they build depends on their culture. In some dry countries, people make homes from mud bricks. In some wet countries, people build homes on stilts to keep the water out.

Culture also affects how people get along. Cultures have different laws, rules, and ways of worship. People from many cultures live in the United States. Some follow the traditions of their ethnic groups. Many ethnic cultures are part of American culture. Americans eat food from Italy. They listen to music from Brazil. They play games from Japan.

Understanding your context means learning the culture around you—the people you are trying to reach. Understanding your context also means knowing the culture you want to develop within the church. As Eric Geiger stated above, if we do not understand the culture we are trying to impact, we are less likely to succeed at our endeavors. .

In Reykjavik, the capital of Iceland, shopkeepers keep their doors closed (It's cold!). But in Telluride, CO most stores keep their doors propped open throughout the winter.

In Japan, the typical household saves three to five times as much of their income as a household in the US. This is not an active decision; it's a cultural component.

These examples show the nuances of a local culture. Knowing the culture you are trying to influence will allow you to understand who they are, what they like to do, what they value, and what offends them.

Creating your church's culture doesn't happen by accident. The truth is, any guest could walk into your church today and ask, "Why do you do that?" (*that* being a program, tradition, practice, use of terminology, music, or just about anything). And you would probably have any number of reasons for an answer. Buried somewhere among your answers would be, "That's just the way we do things around here." Therein lies the simplest definition of culture— *the way we do things around here.*

Sadly, most churches do not create their culture on purpose. Instead, they drift into a culture. But it doesn't have to be that way.

According to Seth Godin, there are two lessons that we can learn about culture in our communities:

> The first is that the easiest thing to do is merely amplify what a culture is already embracing. The second is that real change is cultural change, and you must go about it with the intent to change

the culture, not to merely make the easy change, the easy [sale].

There is another aspect of culture that we need to grasp, and that is the speed at which it is changing. To best realize how the rate of change is accelerating, let's explore how we communicate as a society.

The earliest forms of communication were verbal. We told stories verbally and communicated primarily with words and sounds. Some of the earliest generations of humanity then communicated with pictures and images carved and drawn on cave walls, stones, and wood.

As humanity progressed, the introduction of writing on parchment and scrolls became the medium of choice for those educated and trained to write. There were a couple of serious constraints with this evolution. First, only a select few could read or write. Second, every written document was an original...one of a kind. You could not produce copies without totally re-writing the manuscript. Again, very limiting.

The next major breakthrough in communication was the invention of the Gothenburg Press in 1450 AD and the English language book in 1475. Finally, a way to mass-produce literary works and share them with others.

The arrival of mechanical movable type printing introduced the era of mass communication which permanently altered the structure of society. The relatively unrestricted circulation of information and (revolutionary) ideas transcended borders, captured the masses in the Reformation, and threatened the power of political and religious authorities. The sharp increase in literacy broke the monopoly of the literate elite on education and learning and bolstered the emerging middle class.

The next major milestone in communication was the age of radio, then television, then the Internet, and now mobile computing. Something else is bound to follow. Whatever is next is guaranteed to be faster, smaller, more accessible, and cross all socioeconomic barriers. It is going to be fun to see what it is.

The point here is not technology, but rather the rate of change and how our culture has adapted with these changes. The following is rather stunning:

- Gutenberg Press 1450
- Broadcast Radio 1920: 470 years after the printing press
- Commercial Broadcast Television 1941: 21 years after radio
- Basic Cable Network 1976: 35 years after Commercial Broadcast Television
- AOL 1991
- Google 1998
- YouTube 2005
- Facebook/Twitter 2006
- iPhone 2007
- Android platform 2008
- GPS on Phones 2009

The times between communication mediums are changing and enhancing at an incredible rate. I met a person the other day with a college degree in social media. When I graduated from college in 1984, I did not know how to use a computer and never imagined we would ultimately carry them around in our pockets.

So if the people living in our communities are communicating and doing life differently than they did in the broadcast radio era, how should our churches be adjusting? Let's start by answering that question with vision clarity in the next chapter.

Chapter 14

Vision Transfers through People, Not Paper

In his book, *Church Unique,* Will Mancini describes clarity this way:

> What is Clarity really about? A synthesis of definitions brings clarity to the concept of clarity: it means being free from anything that obscures, blocks, pollutes, or darkens. Being clear as a leader means being simple, understandable, and exact. The leader helps others see and understand reality better. Leaders constantly bring the most important things to light: Current reality and future possibilities, what God says about it and what we need to do about it.

How does that resonate with you? Is your church staff, leaders, and the congregation clear on the "why" of what you do? Without the clarity of direction, people start to question, "What is this all about?" or "Why are we doing this?" or worse, "I sure hope the pastors know what they are doing."

It's far too common. Organizations suffer from a lack of vision clarity either because the leader fails to communicate it effectively or people simply don't trust the leader enough.

Far too many churches think that they have clarity because they have a mission statement. They plaster it on the lobby wall, put it on the website, and cover the back of their business cards all while being totally deceived that they know who they are and why they exist. Yet if you ask them if the community would miss them if they ceased to exist, they cannot respond affirmatively.

Vision statements can be incredibly powerful tools to rally your congregation around your vision and calling, if it really represents the vision. Or they can be unwieldy statements that make people dose off, yawn, and become numb to getting something done. The key is to make your vision statement a call to action rather than a long, descriptive statement.

The Old Testament reveals that whenever people lost sight of the Promised Land, they began to cherish more temporal things like food. They lost sight of the goal and began to focus on immediate gratification. As you read through the Old

Testament, you can feel like you are on a rollercoaster ride. This represents the typical sequence of events in the vision life cycle of the Israelites:

- The Israelites are faithful to God with clarity of purpose.
- Sin enters and doubt begins.
- Multiple wrong visions lead to chaos.
- The people rebel.
- The Israelites are exiled, killed in battle, or some other calamity occurs.
- The people realize that things used to be better.
- Repentance occurs.
- The Israelites return to faith in God with clarity of purpose.
- The cycle repeats.

Did this recurring theme perpetuate itself because God was not clear in establishing His goals and purpose for His people? I don't think so. In most instances, it was people taking their eyes off the vision, and their focus shifted. At times it was the influence of a divisive group of people with ulterior motives. Other times it was the lack of strong leaders. More times than not, it was people allowing external situations to adversely influence them. Instead of being 100% sold out to the vision, they would allow any whim or external influence to derail them.

This same sequence often happens on a personal level and in our churches because of a lack of clarity. We may not be exiled or killed physically, but we can become emotionally and spiritually anemic or worse, become ineffective in reaching our community due to this lack of clarity and focus. Many of you reading this are church leaders, and much of the responsibility of this falls on your shoulders. Do you have vision clarity?

Vision transfers through people and not paper. It is real life interactions that convey and transfer your unique vision to your congregation and your guests. I realize that most guests don't ask questions like, "What is your vision?" Even if unstated, however, most people want to know what a church is all about.

Vision clarity is one of the key factors in determining your backstory. And churches must grasp both their vision clarity and backstory before communicating through their facilities.

Chapter 15

Contextually Traditional

Stories are light. Light is precious in a world so dark. Begin at the beginning. Tell Gregory a story. Make some light.
- Kate DiCamillo, *The Tale of Despereaux*

"The church of God does not have a mission; the mission of God is the church."

I first heard the word "contextual" used several years ago during a one-on-one meeting with Dr. David Chadwick from Forest Hills Church in Charlotte. I had never heard that used in this way. What David explained was that their church was going to approach worship and the preaching of the gospel in a form and methodology that was in context to the current culture. They would not water down the gospel. Rather, they would present it in a way that was culturally relevant.

Over the past couple years I have done a great deal of study and research on the trends in the church and particularly the growing churches. My family attends Elevation Church in Charlotte, NC. The church is less than ten years old and has grown from seven families to over 12,000 people on a weekend. I have had dozens of conversations with other church leaders asking me, "How did they do it?"

I have been looking for a way to explain what I believe is at least one of the reasons for this, not just at Elevation but also at so many other fast growing-churches across America. Yes, there are great communicators from the platform at these churches. Yes, they have great music. Yes, they have been ordained by God for such a time as this. I am not saying that these are not all major factors, but I believe one factor is indicative of the success these churches. They are contextually traditional.

So what do I mean by contextually traditional?

Contextual: These churches know who God has called them to be and whom they are to reach. Let's not confuse this clear identity with just being contemporary or traditional. It's not about loud rock music or an organ prelude. It's not about pews or theater seats. It is about understanding who your church can reach and then doing everything in your power and influence to reach people in that target. Contextual is being true to the vision and mission God has called your church to reach and serve.

Traditional: I'm going to be blunt—there are plenty of examples of churches that attempt to be cool and hip, and yet they do not grow. Why? Too many churches have sacrificed traditional preaching. Sin is still sin. The gospel is timeless. God is unchanging. Life still comes through one person, Jesus Christ. The traditional Truth is still what people need today. Being contextual is not a license to make the culture feel good.

I believe the terms "contemporary" and "traditional" have been over used and abused in some cases—and misunderstood for far too long. Even though I used it above to describe timeless truths of the Christian faith, I detest their use in describing the style or methodology of a local church. Over the past 20 years we have relegated the word "contemporary" to describe church music with drums, guitars and video projectors where the term "traditional" refers to choirs, coats and ties, organs, and hymnals.

When we talk about the various flavors of church styles and methods, I firmly believe that the correct term to use is contextual. I do not believe that the use of any music form or instrumentation or dress code is right or wrong. I would even go so far to say that God does not care which we use. Whether you prefer hymns or haze, the methods prescribed need to enhance and further expand your reach to the community.

Chapter 16

Congruency

Design cannot rescue failed content.
- Edward R. Tufte

Congruency refers to the harmony of agreement. It's a state of being. I just love using this word to describe a church's description of itself compared to their actual performance. As part of my role in developing the right tool for a church to fulfill its vision, I do a lot of "secret worshipper" visits. Our team will embark to experience a church's weekend services, unannounced to the general congregation. Prior to the actual engagement date, I will gather data from the church to get a snapshot of who they think they are. What makes them unique? How would they describe their culture?

So many times I will hear, "We are a friendly church." Or "We make people feel welcome." Then the moment of truth: the site visit. I show up as just a guest. Other than a select few leaders, no one knows me. They do not know if I travelled five minutes or 500 miles to be on their campus. They do not know if I am a believer or one searching. They do not know if I am married, divorced, have kids, just got fired, or any other condition of my life. I then approach the facility and in far too many instances, this "friendly" church is gathered in the lobby in their holy huddles. No one greets me or takes the time to welcome me. And by the way, engaging someone is more than a quick, sweet "Hey y'all."

The congruency breaks down in many of the churches I visit. Who they say they are and who they actually are does not match. They think they are friendly, but they don't escort a guest to a small group classroom. They believe that they love their community, but in reality, they like their "club" and really are not all that interested in shaking things up by having too many outsides interrupt their way of doing things.

The Way Space Speaks

So how do facilities communicate a church's vision? How might a church building be congruent with the DNA of the church culture?

When a guest walks on your campus, the space should amplify the message of the church. This amplification is more than microphones and speakers. The building itself should enhance the vision of the church. I can't tell you the who, the what, and the why of your ministry. Those objectives are unique to each local congregation. What I can communicate to you is the importance of the visual congruence of the built space with the vision of the church. Does the visual match the verbal? For instance, if you say you're a church for young families, but you have expensive décor within reaching distance of a two year-old, then your church is not congruent.

Do you say you are friendly, and yet have inadequate signage to direct guests? Do you preach the message of sacrifice and giving, and yet your facilities are lined with marble floors and opulence? Take a moment and think about what your current church space is saying.

Space speaks. Bruce Miller, lead pastor of Christ Fellowship Church in McKinney, TX sums it up well:

> Space speaks.
>
> I marvel at the amount of verses dedicated to describing the tabernacle and the temple(s).

God created a space for us and is now building another one; spaces that I'm sure tell his story, reflect his character and provide opportunity to serve him.

The Gospel itself is a story -- it's carried in words, songs and in the Lord's Supper and Baptism. Why is there no 'space' tied directly to the Gospel? No temple, no tabernacle, no city, no nation. Does this mean buildings are 'Bad?' Of course not, but it does mean that they are not essential and in fact run a great danger of miscommunicating the essence of Gospel and Church. Buildings serve the purposes of the church to exalt, edify and evangelize. We have three fundamental audiences. Can a building exalt God? Can a space defame or distort God? Can an edifice help or hinder edification? Can a space aid evangelize or detract from it? These are crucial questions for those who raise millions and spend tremendous leadership energy rallying congregations to build spaces.

Have you ever heard a song where the lyrics and the music were totally at odds? It is jarring to hear soothing music for a marital march or conversely rock'in music for a reflective lyric. By analogy spaces that sing a different story that the lyrics of our church are discordant.

Chapter 17

Intentionality

What does it mean to be intentional? When I use this word in conversation, I think of it in these terms:

- On purpose
- Premeditated
- Done with a specific result expected
- Attention to details

These are words and phrases that are totally opposite to concepts such as:

- Do it on the fly
- Let's see what happens
- Make it up as we go
- Hope for the best

Most successful ministry leaders adhere to the first list rather than the latter when planning sermon series, accounting methods, ministry initiatives, music sets, website design, and blogs. They plan. They have an eye on the net result of their plans and goals. They do not leave things to chance. And they, or someone on their team, are paying close attention to every detail.

Was God, when speaking to King Solomon, intentional with the design and construction of the first temple?

Take a couple minutes to soak in the specifics of 1 Kings 6:2-38 (NLT):

The Temple that King Solomon built for the Lord was 90 feet long, 30 feet wide, and 45 feet high. The entry room at the front of the Temple was 30 feet wide, running across the entire width of the Temple. It projected outward 15 feet from the front of the Temple. Solomon also made narrow recessed windows throughout the Temple.

He built a complex of rooms against the outer walls of the Temple, all the way around the sides and rear of the building. The complex was three stories high, the bottom floor being 7 1/2 feet wide, the second floor 9 feet wide, and the top floor 10 1/2 feet wide. The rooms were connected to the walls of the Temple by beams resting on ledges built out from the wall. So the beams were not inserted into the walls themselves.

The stones used in the construction of the Temple were finished at the quarry, so there was no sound of hammer, ax, or any other iron tool at the building site.

The entrance to the bottom floor was on the south side of the Temple. There were winding stairs going up to the second floor, and another flight of stairs between the second and third floors. After completing the Temple structure, Solomon put in a ceiling made of cedar beams and planks. As already stated, he built a complex of rooms on three sides of the building, attached to the Temple walls by cedar timbers.

Each story of the complex was 7 1/2 feet high.

Then the Lord gave this message to Solomon: "Concerning this Temple you are building, if you keep all my decrees and regulations and obey all my commands, I will fulfill through you the promise I made to your father, David. I will live among the Israelites and will never abandon my people Israel."

So Solomon finished building the Temple. The entire inside, from floor to ceiling, was paneled with wood. He paneled the walls and ceilings with cedar, and he used planks of cypress for the floors. He partitioned off an inner sanctuary—the Most Holy Place—at the far end of the Temple. It was 30 feet deep and was paneled with cedar from floor to ceiling. The main room of the Temple, outside the Most Holy Place, was 60 feet long. Cedar paneling completely covered the stone walls throughout the Temple, and the paneling was decorated with carvings of gourds and open flowers.

He prepared the inner sanctuary at the far end of the Temple, where the Ark of the Lord's Covenant would be placed. This inner sanctuary was 30 feet long, 30 feet wide, and 30 feet high. He overlaid the inside with solid gold. He also overlaid the altar made of cedar. Then Solomon overlaid the rest of the Temple's interior with solid gold, and he made gold chains to protect the entrance to the Most Holy Place. So he finished overlaying the entire Temple with gold, including the altar that belonged to the Most Holy Place.

He made two cherubim of wild olive wood, each 15 feet tall, and placed them in the inner sanctuary. The wingspan of each of the cherubim was 15 feet, each wing being 7 1/2 feet long. The two cherubim were identical in shape and size; each was 15 feet tall. He placed them side by side in the inner sanctuary of the Temple. Their outspread wings reached from wall to wall, while their inner wings touched at the center of the room. He overlaid the two cherubim with gold.

He decorated all the walls of the inner sanctuary and the main room with carvings of cherubim, palm trees, and open flowers. He overlaid the floor in both rooms with gold.

For the entrance to the inner sanctuary, he made double doors of wild olive wood with five-sided doorposts. These double doors were decorated with carvings of cherubim, palm trees, and open flowers. The doors, including the decorations of cherubim and palm trees, were overlaid with gold.

Then he made four-sided doorposts of wild olive wood for the entrance to the Temple. There were two folding doors of cypress wood, and each door was hinged to fold back upon itself. These doors were decorated with carvings of cherubim, palm trees, and open flowers—all overlaid evenly with gold.

The walls of the inner courtyard were built so that there was one layer of cedar beams between every three layers of finished stone.

The foundation of the Lord's Temple was laid in midspring, in the month of Ziv, during the fourth year of Solomon's reign. The entire building was completed in every detail by midautumn, in the month of Bul, during the eleventh year of his reign. So it took seven years to build the Temple.

Does that sound intentional to you? It sure does to me. God was quite specific about the size, shape, décor, features, finishes, door material, environmental graphics (What else would you call carvings of cherubim and palm trees?), and the floor plan. It's a tremendous example of how God wants us to be intentional

One of the greatest modern day examples of an organization using their facilities, grounds, and environments to communicate story is the Disney Theme Parks. Do you think they care about the details of the story they want their guest to tell their friends and family after their experience? Do you think they leave that experience up to chance?

Let me give you some examples:

> *Trash Cans*: Did you know that Disney studied and learned that the maximum amount of steps a person will walk to get to a trash can is 30 paces? In order to promote the cleanliness of the park, trash cans are placed no farther than 27 paces away from each other That will keep things clean! And not only that, they are not just trash cans, they are a prop and part of the story.

> *On-Stage/Back Stage*: Disney makes a clear distinction between what people see and what people don't see. This goes back to Walt Disney's desire for Disneyland to be a show. Whenever cast members walk on-stage, the show is on. This distinction continues into how cast members dress and even the conversations they have with other cast members.

Streetscape: Disney knows that most of its guests entering the park are excited to see Sleeping Beauty's castle, which happens to be at the end of Main Street. To enhance this visual, the buildings along Main Street get shorter and the awnings extend out further along down the sidewalk. This makes the castle appear farther away and larger than life. This draws you toward the castle.

Sight, Sounds, Smell, and Texture: When you get near the end of Main Street you are presented with a myriad of options as to where to venture next: Tomorrow Land, Adventure Land, and Frontier Land. With each of these options you will be drawn into a different story. Disney is intentional with the imagery that greets you at the entrance of each land. They use music, sounds, and other audible effects to make your experience congruent with what your eyes see. It then draws you deeper into this story by appealing to your sense of smell and texture.

Creativity is not more expensive. What I have learned by observing numerous churches is that most of these impressions are not much more expensive than their basic counterparts.

Intentionality does not have to equate to being more expensive. The process of being purposeful, thoughtful, and deliberate does not have more dollar signs attached.

Are you leaving your story up to chance? People will say something about you. A story will be created about your church. Will it be a fairy tale or a true story?

Chapter 18

Story vs. Fairy Tale

I suspect that men have sometimes derived more spiritual sustenance from myths they did not believe than from the religion the professed.
- C.S. Lewis

Which do you prefer: a story or a fairy tale? What is the difference? And how do they apply to church facilities?

Story refers to the sequence of events described in a narrative. More narrowly defined, it is the means whereby the narrator (or story teller) communicates directly to the reader.

Stories are an important aspect of culture. Many works of art and most works of literature tell stories. In fact, humanity itself is a story. Owen Flanagan of Duke University writes, "Evidence strongly suggests that humans in all cultures come to cast their own identity in some sort of narrative form. We are inveterate storytellers." We use stories to pass on the past to the next generation or to give instruction.

Story is also used to convey an idea, concept, or precaution. A story can be fiction or non-fiction and can have become embellished over time.

A fairy tale, on the other hand, is a type of short story that typically features folklore and fantasy. Most of the time we refer to them as a type of children's literature. The term is also used to describe something blessed with unusual happiness, as in "fairy tale ending" or "fairy tale romance" (though not all fairy tales end happily). In the vernacular, a fairy tale can also mean any far-fetched story or tall tale.

I like stories, and I like fairy tales. I like to understand the past and the present paradigms and all the things you can learn from a story. I also like getting lost in a good fairy tale. I love fairy tales like *The Lion, Witch, and the Wardrobe*. It is great to become transformed into these make-believe worlds with their unique languages, places, characters, and assumptions.

However, what I do not like is when I think I am observing or participating in a story to learn that it is *only* a fairy tale. I feel betrayed, tricked, or misled. Have you ever read a story and were fully immersed in a theme only to find out that it was not congruent? Bummer! I hate "bait and switch" experiences.

Consider the following word association chart:

Story	Fairy Tale
Non-fiction	Fiction
Real and Authentic	Spectacular, but not real
Sustainable	Straw Man
Draws you in and stays true	Draws you in, but reality falls apart

When it comes to your church facility, is it telling a story or a fairy tale? Is it congruent with who you are? Your vision? Your mission? Your culture? Or will people see your facility, then upon experiencing your interactions, worship experiences, and culture realize that it was just a fairy tale?

Chapter 19

Script Writing

In the world of film, a script is a written work by screenwriters for a movie or television program. In a script, the movement, actions, expression, and dialogues of the characters are narrated. It is the compilation of the components of the end product. A well-written script reveals the author's intentions of the story and identifies the elements that will be required to accomplish the engagement of the observer or reader.

I have found that a script has many components that maintain the story so that it does not become boring, ineffective, or disjointed. Here are the common elements of a script:

- *Time and place*: When is the story set? Where does the story occur?
- *Characters*: What brings them to life?
- *Action*: At what pace is the story being told?
- *Dialogue*: What is to be literally said and figuratively communicated?
- *Plot*: What is the primary reason for the story?

- *Scenes*: What do the events of the story say?

Can you imagine a director telling the actors he wants the cast to develop the story without any dialogue, scenes, plot, or action? The same applies to our church experience for guests. If you tell your parking lot team and greeting ambassadors just to be "friendly," how many interpretations of that do you think you would get? If there is not a script that helps your team know what their role is (character), the reason for the story (plot), what they should be doing and saying (action and dialogue), when it should occur and where (time and place), and in what order (scenes) you will get an inconsistence and incongruent group of individuals—working as individuals—instead of living out intended unified story.

As part of our development process with churches, we ask the leaders to write a script (and multiple scripts per ministry area) of the preferred story for a first time guest. This exercise will do at least 3 things:

1. Clarify what you want accomplished and confirm it is consistent with your vision, mission, and culture.

2. Reveal your current blind spots in relationship to the preferred results.
3. Provide a training tool for your teams, both current and future.

This can be revolutionary for your church. I have seen it transform hospitality teams, parking lot teams, greeters, and overall interaction with guests.

Let me share with you a script from a previous client.

Note how the facility plays a role in this story. As you read, also note three critical points:

- There is a backstory, a context to what is happening in the story.
- The story is specific in action, plot, and a particularly the outcome.
- Each story is unique. You cannot take a story and put your church's name on it. Nobody likes generic stories.

The Journey of the Milestone Family

Matt and Marsha Milestone and their three kids (Millie, Mark, and Marshall) have lived in the Selma area for a while. They have driven by the Oak Hills,

Journey Fellowship campus many times and have seen it from the highway on a regular basis.

Matt and Marsha used to go to church growing up but have not really connected with God consistently since they have been married. Matt grew up Catholic but never really engaged with it. Marsha grew up Baptist and kind of opted out after high school. They have wrestled with their fair share of marital problems, which has left them tired and weary. They go to a church once a year or so but even that is not consistent.

Several of their neighbors have mentioned attending Oak Hills Church and shared their positive experience with it. They seem like down to earth, genuine people, which is different than their memories of church people. Their kids are getting older now. Millie is three. Mark is nine. And Marshall is twelve.

One day Mark has a friend over, and his friend mentions Oak Hills Church and how much he loves going. He says, "Mark, you should ask your mom if you can go to church with us some day." The same day Marshall comes home and says a friend invited him to youth group at Oak Hills.

Matt and Marsha talk about it and decide to take a chance and attend Oak Hills as a family. They are not expecting to have a good experience, but they want to encourage healthy friendships for their children. They get up early on Sunday and make their way to this place called Oak Hills Church.

They drive towards the facility and they notice the clear signs directing them where to park as well as the appealing and casual design and décor elements they had never really noticed before. As they get closer, they see a team of men helping with the parking area. It surprises Matt as he has never seen men lead much at church. As they drive onto the property they are greeted warmly.

They get out of the car and notice the busy parking lot. They notice the other families with kids and think to themselves, "Maybe this won't be so bad; it looks like there may be other people like us here." They approach the building and are warmly greeted by several volunteers and also by some other families who are just showing up as well.

As they walk into the building, one of the greeters introduces himself and says, "Welcome, we are so glad you are here today. You may have been here for years, but I don't think we have met before." Matt and Marsha mention that it is their first time to Oak Hills and the greeter smiles and says, "Great! We are delighted you are here. Why don't I show you around for a moment?"

At that moment the greeter stoops down on one knee and says to Millie, "What is your name?" Millie smiles and shares her name. The greeter then speaks with Mark and Marshall and encourages them about what they are about to experience.

Next the greeter shows them into the coffee house where they see a flurry of activity with lots of people hovering around the coffee area, lots of kids walking around with snacks and donuts, and a variety of people sitting at bistro tables just talking and drinking coffee. They notice the couches, feel the welcoming atmosphere. They begin to feel more at ease.

Then the greeter shows them into the foyer and points out the entrance to the worship center. In the foyer, they again notice the ambiance of the church and continue to feel at home. The greeter engages them in conversation as they show them around, asking about their family and how long they have lived in the area.

The greeter walks them to the children's check-in area and tells them about the great children's ministry at Oak Hills. Matt and Marsha mention that their kids' friends have invited them a few times.

They arrive at the children's check-In counter and the greeter introduces the family to the volunteer who smiles and is glad to see them. The greeter gives them a welcome brochure which is sitting right there on the counter and mentions that this brochure explains a bit about Oak Hills Church.

As Marsha fills out paperwork to get their kids checked in to the system, the greeter takes Matt and the kids and shows them around the children's areas, and they notice how fun and inviting it looks. As they walk back to the check-In counter, Mark notices one of his friends from school is there with their family. Mark and his friend high five and the parents begin to connect with one another about how long they have been attending and how their kids love Oak Hills Church too.

After they check their kids in, they walk Millie to her classroom where a friendly volunteer smiles and greets them. There are other kids playing in the brightly colored room, and Millie jumps right in. Matt and Marsha are nervous but relieved. The volunteer assures them she will keep an eye on Millie as it is her first time.

Matt and Marsha now walk with their two kids towards the worship center. They are pleased to hear about "Family Worship" since they were more nervous about their two older kids having a good experience than anyone else. They are glad to have Mark and Marshall with them for a few minutes as they experience church for the first time in a long time as a family.

As they walk into the worship center, the first thing they notice is the couches, bistro tables, candles, and regular chairs and think to themselves, "This does not feel like the church I grew up in, this feels more like our living room." Another layer of anxiety falls away and they begin to relax even more.

As they find a seat, Mark sees his friend again and waves to him again. They notice Marshall now actually feeling comfortable as well. He is the one they are most worried about since they have had their challenges with their almost teenage son.

About that time, Marshall notices a few people he recognizes from school. He does not say anything but is feeling more comfortable.

Worship begins and the Milestone family has already had a good experience. The parents are hopeful and relaxed. They listen and watch a lot during the worship time. The worship leaders and those making announcements seem genuine, friendly, authentic, and real.

It comes time for communion and the speaker explains what is about to happen. After he prays, they notice people all over the worship center going to the tables, then huddling up for prayer in all kinds of ways. It's a bit different, but they are intrigued. They notice people going for prayer and some giving offerings.

At children's dismissal the children's director encourages all the kids to stand up and head to children's ministry. It seems like a large herd of children stand up from all over the worship center and begin walking out. Mark stands up and walks out as his friend comes his way. Next the children's director mentions junior high is dismissed to the coffee house, and Marshall watches for a minute. He sees a few people he knows, and so he stands up and heads to junior high ministry.

Now comes the meet and greet time and the children's director gives them a topic to speak about with those around them. Everyone stands up and several people speak with Matt and Marsha and welcome them to Oak Hills Church. One couple shares with them that they just started attending a few months ago and talks about how their kids love it.

Now they hear a message via a large video screen. They are kind of skeptical at first, but within minutes the winsome communicator has them engaged, laughing, and they have forgotten all about the screen or that the speaker is not in the room.

The message wraps up and they sense that they need something that is here. They don't know if it is God, friends, community or what it is but surprisingly, they are privately thinking about coming back.

They go pick up Millie, and see many other parents at the pick-up line. They pick Millie up, and she seems happy and has a craft she made for them. The volunteer in the room says, "Millie was great. What a beautiful young girl she is. She had a great time. She was kind of nervous at first, but by snack time she was playing with everyone and having fun." Matt and Marsha appreciate the personal care for their youngest child.

They go pick up Mark, and the elementary area is bustling with kids and parents. As they approach Mark's classroom, Mark sees them and runs up to them smiling. Mark shares how he had a great time. He also introduces his parents to another friend in class who goes to his school. They walk out toward the coffee house and wade through the busting foyer filled with young families. They are feeling more at home all the time when they walk into the coffee house to find Marshall hanging out with some friends as well. Marshall notices them, says goodbye to his friends, and rejoins his family.

As the Milestone family walks out to the parking lot, Matt and Marsha are silent but they listen to their kids saying talking about how much fun they had and how they saw several of their friends from school.

They get in the car and Matt and Marsha say, "It sounds like you had a good time." The kids say they had fun. Matt and Marsha ask if they want to come back and the kids all say yes. It has been a good day. Matt and Marsha are not sure how to process it all but they sense something positive has happened here and they reflect on the faith they had growing up. They sense God doing something, but they are not sure how to put it into words. The church wasn't weird, and their kids had a good time so they decide to return.

On Monday, Marsha gets a phone call from a staff person at the church who thanks them for attending and asks about the kids' experiences. Marsha shares a bit of her story and their unexpected positive experience. The staff person encourages the Milestones to return and offers to meet them at the coffee house the next Sunday. Marsha agrees. Matt agrees. They will return.

Chapter 20

The Building is Just a Tool

It may be that the day of judgment will dawn tomorrow. In that case, we shall gladly stop working for a better future. But not before.
– Dietrich Bonhoeffer

I feel the need for a "time out." Everything that we have addressed above may require a lot of work on your part. It may feel overwhelming. For some, it may feel contrived or manipulated. I assure you that that is not my intent or motivation.

Here is the bottom line. Facilities are merely tools to assist a church or ministry to fulfill its vision. I would be the first to encourage you to first consider if a facility is the right tool. It has been the acceptable fallback for most churches in North America, but is it the right tool? I have taught a seminar for years entitled "Why Build When You Can Grow." Your facilities alone will not make your church grow, and there are some pretty compelling reasons not to invest in more facilities. I encourage every church leader I meet to first consider every possible option to do ministry differently before they elect to build, buy, renovate, or expand.

What are some of the things a church building cannot do? Here are three main things a building cannot do:

1. *A building cannot stimulate growth.* If you are not growing now, then you do not need a building to stimulate growth. People think, well, if we build it they will come. If we build it, it is going to create excitement. If you are not already at a point where your growth is a primary factor for building, then building will not stimulate your growth. We have actually seen instances where the opposite has happened and the building initiative has put the church in decline, because the motives were wrong.

2. *A building cannot improve members' giving to ministry.* Again, if the congregation is not already giving and living of life of generosity, a building project cannot get them to become regular contributors. Now, you might do a campaign, and you might have some people come out of the woodwork to give to a

specific project, but will not cause them to adopt a biblical approach to financial stewardship.

3. *A building cannot motivate people to minister*. If we just had a better building, then our people would do more. No they won't! If you build a building prior to establishing a culture of evangelism, outreach, and service, what they are going to want to do is huddle inside the building. They are not going to want to get out and further the ministry. They are going to want to get inside those four walls and be comfortable in their new digs.

All facilities tell a story, and this story should be congruent and contextual with your vision. I firmly believe that having the right "bait" on the hook can be a positive in using the facility in the art of architectural evangelism. And I have strong convictions that while a building cannot save a single soul, it can be a distraction to a guest that could hinder them from hearing and seeing the word.

But church facilities are still just tools and not the gospel. The building is not the story. The gospel is the story that needs to be told. The problem is that some church buildings don't help tell the story.

Chapter 21

The New Front Porch

Thus far we have explored the concept of story, as well as backstory, and the components that comprise both. Now it is time to explore the essentials of facility storytelling. The story that your guests will recount to their friends, family, co-workers, and neighbors is going to be influenced by several controllable stimuli. As we will see, the experience will be initially impacted prior to your guests ever stepping foot on your campus or in your buildings. It does not matter if your guests received a personal invitation to attend your church or they drove by it, all of them will go to one place first: the Internet. They will seek to learn as much as possible before they commit to attending the first time.

Once they have determined that you are attractive enough from the web, the next greatest impression is influenced by your built and natural environments as well as the personal interactions they encounter. There are a number of moving parts that work independently as well as a collectively to set the tone for this first impression. And a first impression—as many of us know—can be a make or break experience.

Let's jump into the individual pieces of the first impression, beginning with your front porch.

If you lived around the turn of the century, the front porch of the homes, the general store, and local business was a vital part of culture. If you wanted to know what was happening in your community, you could sit out on a front porch and see and hear what was going on. My grandparents lived in an old house in Canton, Ohio with a front porch. I can remember as a boy sitting out there and watching the neighbors interact, watching the "social media" of the day in full action. My grandfather used to take me on a walk up Second Street to the general store that also had a front porch. It's where the town connected and shared experiences.

The front porch was a primary means of gathering information. It is also the place that a "first impression" of something or someone might be developed. If the boys in the rockers said that the new hardware store was a great new addition to the community, your first impression would be positive. The converse would also be true. If you wanted to know what was going on at the local church, you could hear the latest by hanging out on the front porch. Or you would ask your neighbor as you swung on your front porch swing and they played catch with their kids in the street or front yard.

So what about in today's culture? I would suggest that, the new front porch is the Internet, websites, and social media. While the traditional front porch has been decimated by zoning laws, busyness and our desire to hibernate in our suburban settings, we have turned to other means and methods to gain the information that we desire. Like it or not, the new first impression of your church may have little or nothing to do with the preaching, music, friendliness, or denominational affiliation. In fact, more times than not, a first time guest will search Google and see if there are any reviews or good/bad press about the church. From that initial experience, they will make a determination if they will visit or not.

When was the last time you were looking for a good place to have dinner and you searched the Internet before leaving your house or office? Did you open a website to be unimpressed by the presentation and representation of the establishment, so you moved on to another? Whether we like to admit it or not, first time guests, especially non-believers, are consumers. They are shopping for an experience and that experience starts on the web. I understand many churched people don't like to think in these terms, but it's something church leaders cannot ignore.

Story is a huge part of our interaction with people and having a congruent story about or churches starts not at the front door, but at your new front porch, the Internet and your website.

Chapter 22

Bait on the Hook

I ask all of our first time guests why they decided to come to our church and 90% of them said they were driving by and were intrigued by our site and our new building, and that is all thanks to the creativity of Visioneering Studios.
- David Garison
Lead Pastor of Northside Christian Church
Spring, Texas

If you were driving down a road in your town, what kind of building would intrigue you? What would cause you to check it out? When you think about that building, who do you think that building was meant to attract? Who was the primary target to get sucked in by the design and amenities?

For Northside Christian, they designed a building specifically for a thirty-something year-old man. And why would a church focus on that age group and gender? It is actually pretty simple for the leadership at Northside Christian.

They believe that if they can attract men in their mid-thirties, they will likely bring their wife and children as well. In most cases, it is easier to engage the entire family if the husband/father is leading the charge and is compelled to attend.

So what did this church decided to do? They were intentional about communicating a story and message to the people they wanted to attract. They made the conscious decision to put "bait on the hook" as they fulfilled their calling to be fishers of men. The attractional elements of the physical campus was intended to be appealing to those they were trying to reach. If you're going fishing for bass, you would not leave the lure at home. Yes, it is possible to catch a fish on a bare hook, but it's highly unlikely. So why do we think it is wrong to put bait on the hook when we are fishing for souls? While I am in complete agreement that the Holy Spirit moves a person to have faith, God also gave us eyes, ears, noses, and other sensory attributes that He uses to influence us.

For the church pictured above, they decided to use several types of bait with the facility. Here are a few examples:

1. The overall design is that of a lodge. It is very masculine and appealing to a man. It makes me want to go hang out. How about you?

2. The materials are masculine. From the stone to the exposed wood grains to the exposed metal to the car license plates used to clad a section of the facility, the materials appeal to men. Women are generally drawn in by color, but men are attracted to materials.

3. They took the bait on the hook concept and developed a fishing hole in front of the building that is open to the public. They stocked it with fish. Again, the idea is that a thirty year-old man with three kids would bring the kids to the fishing hole.

4. Besides the fishing hole, this church has been deliberate in the location of their exterior public spaces. Even if you are not interested in fishing, you might enjoy a place to sit outside by a gentle waterfall to read. The playground is open to the public, and the outside sitting areas and tables are inviting to anybody just looking for a place to hang and do life with others. In addition, they were

judiciously placed on the front side of the campus so they are visible to people passing by.

Are you ready to go fishing for your community? Is your church more interested in cleaning fish or catching them?

Chapter 23

The Space Between

What would you say if your architect told you he could design a space that is beautiful, functional, and spacious, and it would only be about 10% of the cost per square foot of the typical building? Too often architects forget about a secret weapon. The space between buildings can be an amazing environment.

Great outdoor space can change the entire experience of being on a site and visiting a building. When attention is paid to the arrival sequence from the time you visually see the site, drive onto it, park your car, and walk up to the buildings, you can create an exciting experience out of a typically mundane one. Picture your average big box shopping center on one hand with its sea of parking facing the road and compare that to New Urbanist developments that creatively find a way to stash the cars and move you right into a pedestrian friendly environment.

Make no mistake, cars are a part of American culture, and unless you are in a dense urban environment with good public transportation, which most of the country is not, you are not going to get away from having a significant amount of a site dedicated to parking, but the parking lot doesn't have to be your most prominent feature if you have a good design team.

Throughout history outdoor public space has been the center of community life for people. Whether it was the Greek Agoras, the Italian Piazzas, or the American town square, people have a desire to come together in an environment that is appealing in design, comfortable to hangout in, and where they can enjoy God's creation outdoors.

Even in the harshest environments of extreme cold and extreme hot climates, these spaces are being developed. The weather may not be conducive to outdoor activity every day of the year, but when it's nice these places fill up. Environments don't get much harsher than Chicago, but head out to Navy Pier or Millennium Park on a nice day, and the places are packed with people. If they can develop great outdoor environments in a climate that harsh, then what's your excuse for not doing it on your site?

How much more would it have cost to take all these great outdoor environments and put walls around them, throw on some roofs, and air condition and heat those spaces? Plus how different would they feel? There's a reason no indoor malls are being developed anywhere in the country anymore while open air town centers are popping up everywhere. People like to be outside and developers don't have to build huge enclosed spaces between buildings. It's a win for everyone.

These same concepts can be applied to church campus designs. Churches often get stuck in a rut called "tradition" or "the way it's always been done." With church design that usually means plopping the building down in the middle of the site and then surrounding it with parking, just like the malls and shopping centers do.

Church leaders and church designers could learn some lessons about creating places people enjoy coming to that include great outdoor public spaces that are gifts back to the community. Crossroads Christian Church in Corona, California is a good example of this intentional decision to incorporate pedestrian friendly design features and create interesting and inviting outdoor rooms between the buildings.

If you are a church planter or pastor of a church and you are contemplating your first building project or an expansion of your current campus, wouldn't you want to develop spaces that your neighbors would desire to visit, and that your congregation would enjoy hanging out in between services and during the week? Before you start your next project figure out how to turn your church inside out so passers-by can see community happening right in your front yard every week.

Chapter 24

Seven Seconds: Make the Most of It

Seven seconds: that is how much time you have to make a first impression. Some experts say more, some say less, but most pundits agree that seven seconds is the average time you have to make a first impression. Think about that. That is not much time.

There are dozens of posts on the Internet that will give you hints to best utilize these seven seconds when going to a job interview or making a sales call. But the same principle applies to the guests at our churches. Have you ever thought that your guests are looking at their experience in much the same way they might evaluate a buying decision? Don't get defensive when people enter your facility for the first time with this perspective. This attitude may not be healthy, but it's a reality churches must understand.

So what can you do in those first seven seconds to influence their experience? I actually believe that a guest to your church will have multiple seven second encounters. Below are the areas that I believe are most critical:

1. *The parking lot experience* - We need to be aware that if this is a challenge and their first seven seconds on your site are frustrating, they may not stay. Even if they do stay, then you began the visit with a tone of frustration.

2. *Where do I go now?* - Way-finding and signage are too often underwhelming, which can add to the anxiety of our guests.

3. *What door do I go in?* - Guests do not want to ask questions and do not respond well to facility ambiguity.

4. *The First "Hey."* - The first person to visually, verbally, and physically interact with a guest sets the tone for the entire experience.

5. *We have been preparing for your visit.* - As they step into your facility, will a guest see that you have been intentional about their arrival? Are things clean, neat, inviting, engaging, and well maintained with a sense pride?

Don't squander those seven seconds. Be intentional.
Be deliberate. And be consistent.

Chapter 25

Do Parking Right

In the previous chapter, we learned first impressions are made in as little as seven seconds. It's not much time to impact the thought and emotional reaction of guests. Every touch point during a guest experience has the opportunity to build on the previous interaction, or to destroy it. Every encounter and milestone of this first experience is critical, like building blocks. Without a strong foundation, the rest of the blocks find themselves less stable and tentative.

Assuming your first-time guest has made the conscious decision to pull onto your church campus, the first seven-second encounter will be in your parking lot. The first impression starts at the entrance of the parking lot and may continue until the guest reaches your front door. Too often church leaders think the parking lot is irrelevant and just a place to store the means of transportation used by the congregation. It's a big mistake to believe parking lots have to be mundane spaces.

As you think about your parking experience, there are three things that are foundational aspects of making the first seven seconds in the parking lot as good as possible.

Create a Parking Ministry.

This is a great way to accomplish two significant ministry initiatives for two very different groups. The first group this impacts is obvious: the guest. A vibrant, proactive, enthusiastic, and welcoming group of people can lift your spirits and defuse some of the anxiety that a guest may be experiencing. Seeing happy people waving and smiling has more impact on others than you realize.

The second group that this impacts is your team. Many of the churches we serve have met in schools or other temporary facilities for years -- and now they have a facility to meet. During those years of being a "church in the box," they had set up teams that would show up on Saturday night or Sunday morning at the crack of dawn to set up for worship that day. These people have developed a bond and a kinship that is infectious. The setup team has actually become their small group, and they love doing life together. But what happens when you do not need to setup every week? What do these people do? And let's face it, most of the set team is made of men. I have been on set up teams with guys that were not yet Christ-followers and others that are new followers and others that are more comfortable doing physical labor. Not to provide a similar ministry opportunity once you occupy space that does not require setup robs them of a ministry opportunity that they are comfortable performing. By starting or expanding a parking ministry, you open up a new opportunity for many of these people to serve.

Elevate the Importance of the Parking Ministry.

Do not view the parking ministry as just a functional activity but rather an opportunity to impact people's lives. The parking lot should be blanketed with praying people. It should be the largest prayer chapel on your campus. Help set the tone for the rest of their experience and see what happens.

Function and Safety.

Church parking lots are not like a retail center, even though many designers and civil engineers lay them out as if they were. In a retail or other commercial application, most of the vehicular traffic is spread out over the entire day. Cars pull off and pull on at different times during the day. But a church parking lot is much more similar to an event venue, more like a concert venue or theme park or sports complex. You have a lot of cars trying to enter or exit the site at the same time. And if you have back-to-back worship experiences with fifteen minutes or less between services, you have a real issue. Having a succinct plan for how to best get cars on and off your site will reduce the amount of stress for the drivers, but will also provide a safer environment. If drivers are not attempting to navigate the parking lot on their own, the likelihood of mishaps is greatly reduced. And not just for vehicular traffic, but for pedestrians.

Please do not see your sea of asphalt as just a place to park vehicles but be intentional and make it a safe environment that is bathed in prayer and enhances the experience of your guests.

Chapter 26

Cinderella's Castle

The creative process is also the most terrifying part because you don't know exactly what's going to happen or where it is going to lead. You don't know what new dangers and challenges you'll find. It takes an enormous amount of internal security to begin with the spirit of adventure, discovery, and creativity. Without doubt, you have to leave the comfort zone of base camp and confront an entirely new and unknown wilderness.

- Stephen Covey, *The 7 Habits of Highly Effective People*

When Walt Disney was designing his world-class theme parks, he said that you can get a dog to do what you want in one of two ways: You can take a stick and beat the dog, or you can take that same stick, place a weenie on the end of it and lead the dog. One requires brute force and is not pleasant for the recipient (or the enforcer) while the other creates a sense of anticipation of a treat, a reward. Which would you prefer?

How many of you have been to a Disney theme park? If you have, then you will be able to take this mental journey with me. Close your eyes and image you have just arrived at the park. You have paid the admission and walked through the turnstiles to be greeted by the train station encompassed by the most incredible array of landscaping and the image of Mickey Mouse. They draw you in with a childlike sense of anticipation. "What could be on the other side?" is a common thought that rushes through the minds of even the eldest of guests.

The vine covered train trestle creates a gateway that identifies the start of a truly magical journey. With its magnetism you are sucked in the park and thrust into Town Square. At first glance of your new surroundings, you are faced with so many choices. The fire station with musicians. Or maybe Goofy and Minnie to give hugs. Or possibly see Mickey Mouse himself at the theater. Regardless of which venue, personality, or feature you gravitate to first all roads in Town Square lead to one place, Main Street USA.

As you round the corner from either side of Town Square, you are transformed into Marceline, Missouri, the home town of Walt Disney. You have stepped back in time to the early 1900s, a time of simplicity and an era almost forgotten. Main Street is where turn-of-the-century architecture and transportation bring the small-town Middle America of the early 1900s to life. There are shops, a dentist office (listen for the drilling in the open window), Walt's apartment and so much more. But if you stand anywhere on Main Street and look in the direction of the park, what is the thing that will always catch your eye?

The hot dog on a stick: Cinderella's Castle. It leads all of the park guests in that direction. You do not need a tour guide to tell you where you are heading. You do not need a big flashing neon say that says, "Go to the castle." It is iconic, and it sucks you in. It is almost like a force-field that gets stronger and stronger the closer you get. It is magical. It is intentional. It communicates a story.

Go ahead and open your eyes and let's apply this to our churches. Our campuses and facilities need a draw like Cinderella's Castle. We need these elements that draw people in and tell a story. What if the entrance to your kids environments was designed in such a way that it would be so obvious to a guest that they would immediately venture to that area, without a sign or someone telling them where to go, the entrance would shout kids come here.

Now, I am not suggesting you do not have signs or greeters. What I am suggesting is that the experience for the guests will be enhanced by providing other visual clues to communicate the story.

Be creative.

Be intentional.

Provide the environment for life change to occur for your guests. Disney is selling the "Happiest Place on Earth." But the church has the greatest Gift this world will ever know.

Chapter 27

Which Way Do I Go?

Think back to a time where you entered a large organizational complex for the first time. Hospitals, high rises, university buildings, sports venues, and airports have one thing in common—people get lost in their mammoth footprints. Clear signage is a necessity, especially for people finding their way in a large facility for the first time.

I spend a fair amount of time on the road. I am in and out of airports, rental cars, and hotels on a weekly basis. I may be in two or three different airports in a single week. I am so thrilled that smart phones have GPS—man's best friend when you are on the road. But I have learned that the GPS does not work very well inside the airport when I am trying to navigate my way to destinations within the terminal. However, most airports use the same, or very similar, iconic signs that allow me to find my way to key landmarks.

There are three signs that put me at ease and make me feel like "I can do this," even if I have never been to that airport. Can you visualize these three signs?

- Men's Restroom (always welcome after a long flight)
- Rental Car
- Baggage Claim

I can follow these signs and not look like that first-time traveler. I can proceed with confidence that I will be able to locate the restrooms and rental cars. These are all examples of way-finding.

In laymen's terms, way-finding elements help lead a guest through the maze of a facility.

These elements can take the form of signage, floor markings, pathways, visual graphics, and even sound and smell. Any element that provides a sensory clue to a desired location can be considered way-finding.

These elements are not for your current attendees. Way-finding is for those not yet at your church, your guests. By providing way-finding—starting at the entrance of your parking lot and continuing throughout the campus experience—you reduce a portion of the walls that a first time guest may have erected. They are able to navigate the parking lot, the pedestrian access points, and circulation spaces without feeling and looking like "that first time traveler."

In addition, way-finding done right can be the landmarks for connection. "Hey Sam, I will meet you outside the double door with the large orange KID CITY sign." These way-finding elements become part of the fabric of your campus, your culture, and your guest's experience. Don't see them as just signs or directional components. See them as part of how your facility tells the unique story of who you are and what you value.

Chapter 28

Environmental Graphics and Storytelling

Everything is design. Everything!
— Paul Rand

For some of you, the term "environmental graphics" may be foreign or one that you have not heard used in a church context.

In short, environmental graphics address the visual aspects of way-finding, communicating identity & brands, information descriptors, and shaping a sense of place. The word *environmental* refers to graphic design as part of creating the built environment, not to the natural environment. So this has little or nothing to do with "environmentalism."

For many church leaders, when they hear this term, immediately think, "kid's theming." You have probably seen the planes hung or half a fire truck that looks like it is driving through the wall or Noah's Ark with animal heads peering through portholes. And while those are definitely a component of this subset of storytelling, it is not the only area of your campus where environmental graphics convey *story*. In fact, I believe that it is a little disingenuous to have an over-the-top children's building while the rest of your campus is sparse. I understand that your target market may be families with young kids, so having a top-notch children's facility is congruent with your vision. But don't forget their parents, your guests.

Environmental graphics are not just for church. One of the best examples of environmental graphics is Hilton Garden Inn.

Have you ever noticed a theme throughout their hotels? They are communicating a story about a garden. Their tag line is "Welcome to the Garden." The story starts as you approach the front door and enter the lobby, even the carpet in the corridors has the same story telling theme. In keeping with this story, their logo on their website has a vine growing. All of the visual elements above, and so many more, are examples of environmental graphics that help communicate a story. I can assure you, that as a weary traveler, when I see the images of vines growing on the front door, or the park like setting off the lobby, I begin to relax and become transformed mentally and emotionally. These kinds of customer-centric businesses know that the environment and the sense of place is an asset to their guests. They have been intentional about setting an environment that is welcoming, warm, and familiar, all while communicating a story that guests relate to and regulars are comforted by.

Our guests see these kinds of environments in many of the places they hang out and visit. It is part of their everyday life and culture. The church should not reflect the world, but let's not be so different in our built environments that guests are put off before they ever have a chance to hear the good news of Christ. Being intentional with creating an environment is as critical as determining how many seats you need in the worship center. Don't miss this opportunity to impact people.

What the Apple Store Tells Us about Humanity

The story a building tells only goes so far. Without the human element to augment the facility story, life change is much less likely to occur. In fact, great churches can exist in poor facilities because of the people. The human element will always trump the built space. At the same time, the opposite can occur. Have you ever been to an incredible hotel or restaurant, sucked in by the physical appeal and ambiance, only to be turned off by the way a person treated you?

The same applies at our churches. People make the story appealing, or they can totally erode all of the other efforts you have invested to tell your story.

There are many obvious human touch points that will impact your guests. We have discussed the parking lot ministry and how incredibly important it is with establishing that first impression. The greeters are the next obvious touch point. Are they warm, welcoming, engaging, not too overbearing, and informative? Are they there only to hand out the worship guide or are they to impact people? Don't forget to write a script for this area of your ministry just like we did for the first time guest with kids or the parking lot team. Determine what defines a win for that group of ambassadors of your story. They are not just greeters; they are the initial face of your story.

Let's compare the typical church interaction with how they do it at the Apple Store.

Many churches that we work with will tell us that they want a "Welcome Center Booth" or a kids check-in counter. In most cases they are envisioning a counter with their volunteers and/or staff on one side and the nervous and intimidated guest on the other side. I hate this setup. This creates such an "Us vs. Them" visual barrier, and not just visual, it can taint the interaction. This kind of arrangement generally requires the guest to start the conversation instead of the host, which is completely backwards. The host should be engaging and trying to build a relationship while initiating a conversation.

Have you ever been to an Apple Store? Throughout the majority of the store, what is missing? Counters!

Most of their products are out on tables or displays with theirstaff roaming the store, engaging guests, and physically demonstrating the product for customers. Imagine having a group of ministry ambassadors floating around the kid's check-in area looking for guests, cladded in colorful shirts, and armed with answers for guests? What if they approached a guest and instead of telling them they had to fill out a card, the ministry volunteers pulled out their iPad and started a conversation with some leading questions that helped them complete the normal registration process. Would that be more inviting to a guest? It would for me.

Not only are you obtaining the data that you need as a church, but you have now connected to people in community. That guest will feel like they know somebody so it will be less awkward next week. The personal interaction has now reinforced the story of the built environment.

The Apple Store reminds us that human interaction trumps everything. Does your facility space help tell the story or human interaction or hinder it?

Chapter 30

The Forgotten Issue: Facility Condition

Have you ever walked into a restaurant that you read about online or someone recommended—full of anticipation and excitement—only to then be turned off by the lack of care of the facility? I have been disappointed more times than I can recall by dirty facilities. What message does a dirty church convey to a first time guest? Not a great witness in my opinion.

In his book *First Impressions*, Mark Waltz addresses what it is like to be a guest in our churches and how the first impression may not always be the best. In addition, the first impression may be the only chance we have to impact their lives. He writes, "When your guests are distracted from the real purpose of their visit to your church, you'll have a difficult time re-engaging them. In order for people to see Jesus, potential distractions *must* be identified and eliminated."

Have you ever considered that the condition of your buildings could affect your ability to engage and minister to people? Most of our previous chapters have focused on the physical attributes related to the built environment. We have looked at the design, the way-finding, and other attributes of the campus and structures. But what about the condition?

Over my 28-year career of planning and building churches, ministry and educational facilities, I have witnessed firsthand the use, abuse, and misuse of ministry facilities. I have seen churches spend millions of dollars on new facilities and then neglect to change the HVAC filters, repair leaks, change light bulbs, and caulk annually as required. We must act responsibly with our church facilities. Ultimately, they are not our buildings. They are God's buildings.

I find that many church members take better care of their homes, boats, cars, motorcycles, and even their pets than they do their ministry facilities. Is this acceptable to you? I believe that God holds each of us responsible and accountable for what we do and how we handle every resource entrusted to us.

When I was in my early years of college I took a two-year sabbatical to travel with a musical group out of Nashville called Bridge. We did over 350 concerts a year, traveling from town to town and church to church. Every night we did a concert in a new location, and so we set up and took down our sound system each night. We had wires going everywhere. So to dress up the stage and to make it safe to navigate the performance area, we used duct tape to secure the wires. We bought the stuff a case at a time. I even had to repair a pair of pants, due to an attire malfunction, with duct tape until we could locate a seamstress. It is the dream product for repairing and securing just about anything.

But after our concerts each night, we pulled up the duct tape and threw it away. It did not stay as a permanent part of the décor of the church. It was installed and removed the same day because it was never intended to be a permanent fixture in the facility. However, I cannot begin to tell you how many times I visit a church that has elected to use duct tape as a permanent component of their interior design scheme. The congregation steps over the duct tape week in and week out totally oblivious to the grey stripe on the worn-out carpet.

The longer you live in a space, the less you see the obvious. For your regular attenders, they become immune to the condition of the facility. We stop seeing the trees for the forest. We walk past the grass growing in the cracks of the parking lot. We step over the torn carpet. We know exactly how to avoid the potholes in the parking lot. We do not notice the stained ceiling tiles and overlook the odor and condition of our public restroom. But I assure you, your guests will notice. These inconsistencies in the story can be just as distracting and repulsive as poor design and the lack of signage and poor interactions.

The condition of your facility will speak volumes to guests. It will communicate what the church values, which may be an indicator of how a guest may be treated as well. As a guest to dozens of church facilities a year, the condition of the space and campus are first clue indicators to me as to what is important to that congregation or the leadership. While it may not always be indicative of the desired culture, vision, and mission of the church, it is an indicator that will influence my overall impression.

This past year our team attended two conferences at large influential churches. The first was a church in Southern California with a campus that is the best keep facility I have ever visited. It has a half dozen buildings uniquely located on a 50-acre site. When you first pull on the property, you are greeted by signage at nearly every intersection of the parking lot to guide you to your destination. The grounds were immaculately manicured and all the hedges trimmed and neat. The buildings were clean and organized, lacking disruptive clutter in the common areas. The restrooms were neat, clean, and odor free. The place was not opulent, but comfortable. The windows and glass were clean. And no duct tape on the floor!

The other conference was in central Florida at a very large church. This is a church with an impactful TV ministry in central Florida and dynamic pastor. The conference had over 5,000 people in attendance, so this was no small campus. But I was very disappointed with the condition of the facility. The signage on the campus was lacking, and a significant amount of the parking was gravel.

As I approached the buildings, after parking in the gravel lot, I was immediately disappointed by the lack of care of the grounds. The yards were in desperate need of care, and the trees and shrubs needed a good trim. The building felt old and tired, lacking any visual appeal. Then I ventured deeper into the campus. Pathways led me to the sea of modular classrooms. In fact, the speaker's lounge was in one of these spaces, which gave the impression that "OK" was good enough for them. There was no sense of excellence or intentionality to the space. Touring the actual worship center revealed aged and worn pews, carpet that was wrinkled, and restrooms that really could have used some TLC.

Now, I can still worship and enjoy my time with other believers in such a space. But what about our guests, especially those who are not believers? Will they be as forgiving? Will the condition of our facilities leave a lasting negative impression on them? Will these roadblocks keep them from coming back or sharing their experience with others?

Don't let the condition of the facility be the forgotten chapter in the story of your church.

Chapter 31

The Cost of Getting It Wrong

Most churches we partner with or serve in some capacity are usually focused on making decisions to address an immediate need. Whether that is financing, staffing, space/facilities or other ministry initiatives, they have a pain point. They need a solution, so they commit their energies and efforts to addressing those immediate issues. This is understandable, and I would even suggest it is needed. A natural progression in this process is for church leaders to start thinking about the cost of the decision they are wrestling with. What will the right salary package be for this position? What is the interest rate and closing costs of the loan? Will we have to hire additional staff to accomplish the ministry initiatives? What is the cost of a new or renovated facility? These are all viable questions to consider.

However, the questions too often over looked are "What if we get it wrong?" and "What will it cost us if we don't get this right?"

These questions are not meant to paralyze leadership or to stymie a decision, but rather to help a church not commoditize these critical decisions. Think about these questions in the following contexts: What will it cost if you make a bad hire? Not just in the terms of monetary, but in poor performance, opportunity costs, corrective measures, and emotional energies.

What will it cost to have the wrong audio and acoustics in your worship center? Again, this is not just the cost to fix the issue, but the frustration quotient and emotional capital. What are they worth?

What is the cost if you use facility components that are inefficient and run up energy costs and have shorter life cycles? Keep in mind that 70 to 80% of the total cost of facility ownership over a 40 year period is associated to facility operations. And those costs are at inflated rates for the life of the facility.

What if the design and construction is wrong? What if the facility does not appropriately convey your unique story? What if the facility is not flexible to accommodate changes in your ministry initiatives in the future?

It is far too easy and common for church leaders to turn these critical decisions into a commodity. Let's look back at the first bullet above. When you are looking for a candidate to fill a new position, does the following play into the discussion: "We will hire the person with the lowest salary requirements." I would bet your answer is "no." That does not mean that you select the highest paid candidate either. What you really want is the right person on the bus. And when we look at decisions with that as a primary lens, we tend to make better decisions. Might we pay some percentage higher than the lowest salary range candidate—yes, but what is the total cost of that lower paid person if they are not effective?

When we look at the total cost of facility ownership, we see that the cost of "sticks and bricks" is only about 20% of the total life cycle cost, and the cost of the architect and contractor is only about 3%. Even with this knowledge in front of us, we tend to look for ways to reduce the design cost or the builder's profit margin. We try to lower the smallest piece of the total cost of facility ownership, which in turn can drive up the largest portion of the life of the facility as well as having the likely potential of having a facility that is not congruent with our story, vision or mission.

No, buildings are not everything. But they are important. And more times than not, church leaders fail to see the importance of the buildings and the stories they tell.

As you have seen throughout this book, buildings are more than just physical facilities. They tell stories. They welcome guests. They can take down the barriers for persons to hear the gospel. They can be a place where a hurting person finds healing.

So . . . what is the cost of getting *that* wrong?

About the Author

Tim Cool has assisted more than 350 churches (equating to over 4 million square feet) throughout the United States with their facility needs. He has collaborated with churches in the areas of facility needs analysis, design coordination, pre-construction coordination, construction management and life cycle planning/facility management. In addition, as a former Visioneer with Visioneering Studios, Tim was able to refine concepts related to facility "Story-telling", place making and other similar topics leading to a number of the concepts found in this book.

Tim has also been a conference speaker at numerous national conferences and seminars including the national conferences for the NACBA, NACFM, Texas Ministry Conference and Worship Facility Expo. He maintains his national membership with the International Code Council for building codes. He is also a member of the International Facility Managers Association, National Association of Church Business Administration and National Association of Church Facility Managers.

Tim is also the author of the book, *Successful Master Planning: More Than Pretty Pictures*. He has been married to his best friend, Lisa, for 29 years and resides in Charlotte, NC with their 17-year-old triplets. They are active members at Elevation Church.

Contact Information:
http://coolconversationslive.com
(704) 507-8672

Made in the USA
San Bernardino, CA
11 April 2015